The Laurel Classical Drama has as its purpose the presentation of a representative selection of the major tragedies and comedies of ancient Greece and Rome. The masterpieces of Aeschylus, Sophocles, Euripides, Aristophanes, Menander, Plautus, Seneca, and Terence appear in translations chosen for their freshness and readability.

ROBERT W. CORRIGAN is Rackham Professor of English at the University of Michigan. He was the first President of the California Institute of the Arts. Formerly, he taught drama at Carleton College, at Tulane University, and at the Carnegie Institute of Technology, where he was an Andrew Mellon Professor and head of the Department of Drama. He was also Professor of Dramatic Literature and Director of the Program in the Arts at New York University. He founded and edited the *Tulane Drama Review*. He is editor of *Theatre in the 20th Century*, *The Delta New Theatre of Europe* series, *The Laurel Classical Drama* (5 vols.), and *The Laurel British Drama*. He is the author of *The Theatre in Search of a Fix*.

The Laurel Classical Drama

AESCHYLUS

THE ORESTEIA TRILOGY

    1 *Agamemnon*
    2 *Choephoroe*
    3 *Eumenides*

PROMETHEUS BOUND

EURIPEDES

THE BACCHAE
HIPPOLYTUS
ALCESTIS
MEDEA

GREEK COMEDY

ARISTOPHANES

    Lysistrata
    The Birds
    Peace
    The Plutus

MENANDER

    The Grouch

Sophocles

The Laurel Classical Drama

OEDIPUS THE KING

PHILOCTETES

ELECTRA

ANTIGONE

in modern translations

edited, with an introduction,

by Robert W. Corrigan

Published by DELL PUBLISHING CO., INC.
1 Dag Hammarskjold Plaza, New York, N.Y. 10017
© Copyright, 1965, by Dell Publishing Co., Inc.
Laurel ® TM 674623, Dell Publishing Co., Inc.

ISBN: 0-440-38154-1

Printed in U.S.A.
Grateful acknowledgment to the following for the
translations used in this volume:

Michael Townsend for his translation of ANTIGONE.
Copyright © 1962 by Chandler Publishing Co. Reprinted
by permission of Mr. Townsend. Performance rights for
this version should be obtained from Michael Townsend,
The Firs, Lyddington, Nr. Uppingham, Rutland,
England. No performance may take place unless
a license has been obtained.

Kenneth Cavander for his translations of OEDIPUS THE KING
and PHILOCTETES. Copyright © 1962 by Kenneth Cavander.
Application to publish or perform his versions of
these plays should be made to Margaret Ramsay, Ltd., 14
Goodwin's Court, London, W.C. 2, England. No publication
or performance may take place unless a
license has been obtained.

Francis Fergusson for his translation of ELECTRA,
reprinted by permission of the translator and New
Directions, Norfolk, Connecticut. Copyright
1938 by William R. Scott Co.

Contents

Introduction 11

ANTIGONE 29
translated by Michael Townsend

OEDIPUS THE KING 67
translated by Kenneth Cavander

ELECTRA 127
translated by Francis Ferguson

PHILOCTETES 175
translated by Kenneth Cavander

Introduction

THE TRAGIC TURBULENCE OF SOPHOCLEAN DRAMA

Robert W. Corrigan

Sophocles, alas, has been allowed to become a cultural monument. In contrast to Euripides, whose atonalities seem so akin to those of the mid-twentieth century, Sophocles is usually thought of as the poet of serenity, the champion of self-restraint, and the hero of a hard-won spiritual peace. His plays are hailed as great landmarks of balance and harmony, in which form and idea are perfectly conjoined. Like Goethe, Mozart, and Dante, he is a classic; and as such he is taught and revered, but seldom—at least not in the theatre—are his plays enjoyed as living works of art. With a few exceptions, notable in their rarity, most productions of Sophocles' plays with their hollow ranting, posturing gestures, wooden movements, and Old Vic-ish choruses are dreadfully dull. The prevailing attitude seems to be: "By all means, let's teach Sophocles in school, but if we must have Greek drama in our theatres let's do one of the modern versions—preferably French—such as Anouilh's *Antigone,* or Giraudoux's *Electra;* or, if we are going to be really experimental, we'll try Cocteau's *The Infernal Machine.*" To think this way is to do both ourselves and Sophocles a disservice, and, more important, it in no way takes into account the generative power of the Greek theatre. Sophocles can stand such a misunderstanding, but we suffer a profound cultural loss that is as unnecessary as it is dangerous. In order to avoid this, I share William Arrowsmith's belief that the first obligation of the scholars and critics of Greek literature is to help us regain that sense of vitality and turbulence—Arrowsmith's "the turbulence of experience, and the turbulence of ideas under dramatic test"—which made Greek drama exciting theatre. We must discover ways to restore for both readers and audiences the dynamics of Greek drama in production (Artaud referred to it as "the physics of Greek tragedy"); and more particularly we must find the means that will encompass that turbulence which we know must have characterized the plays of Sophocles when they were first produced in the fifth century B.C.

If we are to be successful in this, I believe that from the very beginning we must refrain from our tendency to categorize Greek drama and should acknowledge the futility of searching for an "idea of Greek tragedy." It is a commonplace that Aristotle's famous definition of tragedy is not descriptive of the majority of the 33 extant plays. And the more recent theories, such as "with purpose, through passion, to perception" or the ritualistic-origins approach, are equally inadequate. Even a structural definition proves unsatisfactory as soon as one attempts to make it into a generalized principle. What formal consistency does one find when he compares *Antigone* to *Oedipus Tyrannus,* or to *Electra,* or *Oedipus at Colonnus?* (Not to mention trying to compare the plays of Aeschylus and Euripides in terms of structure!) For the Greeks of the fifth century, as Professor Norman J. Dewitt has so persuasively demonstrated, a tragedy (a "goat song") was "any play based upon the legends of the historical aristocracy" performed at the festivals of Dionysus. It may very well be true that these festival performances originally had religious and ritual significance, and this may account for certain common conventions shared by each of the playwrights; this fact may even explain why certain plots and themes were continually used; but by the time of Sophocles the Dionysian festivals had lost most of their religious significance and drama had moved from the realm of religion to that of art, hence the ritual origins of the Greek theatre are of little or no help when it comes to understanding the meaning, significance, or dynamic of any one play. In the end, formal explanations of Greek drama are as limited and limiting as the more popular thematic approaches.

It seems to me that a more effective way of dealing with

the problem would be to distinguish between *the form of tragedy*, which constantly changes—even in the work of a single dramatist—and *the tragic*, which is a way of looking at experience that has persisted more or less unchanged in the Western world from the time of Homer to the present. Santayana once wrote: "Everything in nature is lyrical in its ideal essence, tragic in its fate, and comic in its existence." The tragic writer in all ages has always been chiefly concerned with man's fate and a man's fate is that he is ultimately doomed to defeat because he is born to die. Aeschylus, Sophocles, and Euripides were tragedians because they, for the most part, were concerned with the individual's struggle with Fate; and for them, as for all Greeks of the fifth century, this struggle is seen as a conflict with necessity (*anankē*). Necessity is not some kind of social disease that those who would change the world can ignore, soften, or legislate out of existence. Necessity is the embodiment of life's smallness, absurdity, and fragility; it is the acknowledgment of the limitation and mortality of all human experience. Man's struggle with necessity has been expressed in many forms and in varying contexts throughout history, but it is the constant of tragic drama, and it is the bond that links the three writers of classical Greek tragedy insofar as they can be related. It is the presence of the tragic sense of life in two such different plays as *Oedipus Rex* and *Hippolytus* that justifies *our* calling them tragedies, while we rightly consider *Alcestis* and *Helen* (plays in which the force of necessity has been suspended) as romantic comedies, despite the fact that the Greeks thought of them—or at least called them—tragedies.

The tragic view of life, then, begins by insisting that we accept the inevitable doom of our Fate, and this fact is the mainspring of all tragic drama. However, our experience of tragedy tells us that it is more than this. The great tragedies of history also—and with equally compelling force—celebrate the fact that, while a man may have to learn to face and accept the reality of necessity, he also has an overpowering need to give a meaning to his fate. If man's fate, no matter how frightening, has no meaning, then why struggle? "If," as Kierkegaard wrote in *Fear and Trembling*, "there were no eternal consciousness in a man, if at the foundation of all there lay only a wildly seething power which writhing with obscene passions produced everything that is great and everything that is insignificant, if a bottomless void never satiated lay hidden beneath all—what then would life be but despair?" But, like Prospero, we tend to trust that our ending is not despair, and our experience with tragic drama is sufficient testimony to our capacity to struggle against and give meaning to our Fate.

The spirit of tragedy, then, is not quietistic; it is a grappling spirit. But the nature of the struggle varies in direct relationship to the individual dramatist's belief in the meaning of the struggle. In the plays of Aeschylus, for example, the heroes struggle, but finally the gods must enter in and resolve it. Euripides' characters, on the other hand, usually don't struggle to do something so much as they try desperately and futilely not to do something. But either way, they tend to emerge as victims, for seldom, if ever, are they capable of imposing a meaning on their Fate. Only in the tragedies of Sophocles do we sense the validity of a meaningful struggle and the real possibility of it. His characters may win or lose; or more exactly, they win in the losing and lose in the winning. But it is the struggle itself that is the source of the dramatic significance, and it is out of this struggle with necessity that heroism is born.

Here, again, Aristotle—or at least the usual interpretations of *The Poetics*—has misled us. That quality of the will in human nature which dares to struggle with necessity is called *hubris* by Aristotle, and is described in *The Poetics* as a flaw and a horrible thing. We must never forget that this interpretation of *hubris* is an expression of the fourth century's admiration (or need) for moderation in all its forms, and while the turmoils of the fifth century may have prompted the widespread acceptance of such an attitude, to apply it as a judgment or think of it as descriptive of what happens in classical tragedy is nonsensical. For Sophocles, at least, *hubris* is that quality in man which defies the *status quo* of being human; it is the protest against the limitations of being a man. And whether this resistance takes the form of an inordinate and monomaniacal pursuit of a finite goal, or is the arrogant and suicidal aspiration toward the infinite, it cannot be considered as only a character defect of egotism. Rather, it is an integral part of human nature; it is the necessary counterpart of man's capacity as a feeling and thinking being. This explains why the action of tragedy seems creative and destructive at the same time, why the spirit of tragedy is the spirit of achievement. It is an end (death) and it is a fulfillment, a complete realization filled with a heightened sense of life.

It is the paradoxical nature of this confrontation with Fate which leads the hero into what Karl Jaspers has called "boundary situations," those areas of experience where man is shown at the limits of his sovereignty. "Here," as Richard B. Sewall puts it in his *The Vision of Tragedy,* "with all the protective coverings stripped off, the hero faces as if no man had ever faced it before the existential question—Job's question, 'What is man?' or Lear's 'Is man no more than this?' " At this frontier, the hero with faith and those generalizations derived from his experience attempts to map his universe. Finally, what happens in tragedy is a failure of maps. In the tragic situation, man finds himself in a primitive country that he had believed his forefathers had tamed, civilized and charted, only to discover they had not. One of the great holds that tragedy has always had on the imagination is that it brings us into direct touch with the naked landscape. The playwright begins by moving the hero into the destructive element, and then he presses these boundary situations to their fullest yield. In the midst of "the blight man was born for," the tragic dramatists demands of his hero what Conrad Stein has called: "How to be!" Thus, in carrying the action to the uttermost limits, the playwright is able to explore the farthest reaches of human possibility.

Man's tragic condition is that he is doomed by Fate to defeat. The affirmation of tragedy is that it celebrates a kind of victory of man's spirit over his Fate. This mortal encounter between the tragic and tragedy—between life and form—is the chief source of tension and turbulence in what we call tragic drama. In the ambiguity of that tension, death in some form usually triumphs, but heroism is born out of that mortal struggle and its spirit lives on long after the corpse has been interred.

The failure of most interpretations of Sophocles' plays is the total disregard for the turbulence of this tension. In much the same way as the Bible has been devitalized by the petty moralizing of most Sunday school stories, the critic, in his need to clarify, tends to oversimplify and thus destroys that marvelous rage of the blood which courses through the plays. Most interpretations of *Antigone*, for example, usually pit a noble Antigone fighting in behalf of a belief in the traditional gods (divine law) against a hardhearted, tyrannical Creon who stands for social and political order (human decrees). First of all, such an abstract formulation is woefully superficial, but more important, it can never be a dramatic *action;* it captures none of the strife and internal struggle of the play; it is incapable of expressing the dividedness of belief, and, at best, it can only produce a cheap kind of political melodrama.

Rather than seeing Antigone and Creon in dialectic opposition to each other, we should stress their similarities, remembering that they are of the same family and share a common fate, remembering also that Sophocles—contrary to the assertions of some commentators—never conceived of action in terms of the Hegelan dialectic. The most frightening and morally significant struggles in human life are usually those in which the opposing forces use different means to achieve similar ends in the name of identical values. One need only read the speeches, attacks, and counterattacks in our newspapers to realize that the current struggle between the United States and Russia is of this nature. The labels may be different, the ideologies may seem to be at odds, but both sides claim to be fighting in the cause of freedom; each is striving to free the world from domination by the other. We find a similar condition in the regular flare-ups between big business and the labor unions (which are also big business): both sides in these disputes are seeking greater prosperity, and each claims to be working for the general good of society. People become dramatic when they insist on acting on their beliefs. Dramatic action is the collision of people acting in this way, but dramatic action does not become morally significant until this conflict is fought under identical banners of value.

What distinguishes Antigone and Creon is not principle, for they both claim to act in behalf of love. They are in conflict only insofar as they are both caught up in the family's common fate. What is significant is what happens to them as they fulfill their destinies, as they struggle to give a meaning to their fate. Antigone, in her steely assertion of the principle of love, nearly destroys her own humanity (and thus her capacity to love) and denies the presence of love in others. Her greatness resides in her capacity—in the nadir of loneliness—to push the principle beyond the point of denial to the place of rediscovery— rediscovery of love and her own humanity.

Creon never reaches this stage of self-discovery. He suffers just as much as Antigone, actually more; but because he is morally blind he lacks the capacity and the drive to force his fate to its fullest yield. To the very end of the play he sees himself as a man who has struggled hard for the cause of justice in the name of love, only to suffer the misfortunes of a fickle fate. Creon is a man of intelligence, shrewdness, and strong resolve, but he lacks the humanity necessary to understand his fate. Because of this incapacity he is a victim and therefore can know only the horror of his fate. Antigone's capacity for a greater humanity is the source of heroism, and while this heroism in no way softens her fate, it does give it a glory that all men aspire to, but few ever achieve.

In this regard, I believe Arrowsmith is absolutely correct when he writes about the play as follows:

> What she [Antigone] first accepts as a fate, the principle of love that dooms her to death, is hardened by her desperate plight and her desperate courage and loneliness; and this in turn hardens her—"Great suffering makes a stone of the heart," as Yeats put it— making her refuse Ismene the same dignity of fate she claims. As she hardens, so does Creon on behalf of the same principle, denying Haemon in order to hurt Antigone, just as Antigone dishonors Ismene in order to honor Polyneices. Still hardened, but in-

creasingly tormented by a loss she does not understand and yet the fate she chose, Antigone is condemned to her symbolic death, walled alive in a tomb,
and thus cut off alike from both the living and the
dead, the human being still alive, like Niobe, beneath the cold rock of her heroism. And suddenly,
as the chorus compares her to a goddess, she knows
what has happened, and cries, "I am mocked, I am
mocked!" and the rock falls away, leaving that final
warm confusion that makes her so human and so
lovely.*

The play's turbulence resides in this: each of the characters in the play acts on behalf of the principle of love,
but the common fate of Antigone and Creon is that to hold
steadfast in the cause of love they must deny others the
right to love. Each, insisting that he be allowed the dignity
of shaping his own fate, must deny this right to others.
Antigone's heroism is born when she, in the moment of
agony, discovers her failure as a woman and is thus able
once again to reassert that humanity which gives meaning
and vitality to the principle itself.

There is a similar turbulence to be discovered in Electra's
waiting as she endures the ravishing delays of a god not
ready to act, or in the persuasions of Neoptolemus and
Odysseus as they try to seduce Philoctetes into rejoining
the Greek forces at Troy. However, in the rest of this introduction I should like to focus my attention on *Oedipus
the King*, probably the greatest, most difficult, and most
mysterious of all the existing Greek tragedies. This is not
the place for a detailed analysis of the play, but I hope my
remarks will at least be preliminary soundings that can begin to express that quality of turbulence which drives this
great play.

Oedipus the King is usually thought of as one of the
world's great detective stories. Oedipus, the great sleuth,
the one who has solved the inscrutable Sphinx's difficult

*William Arrowsmith, "The Criticism of Greek Tragedy,"
The Tulane Drama Review, Volume III, No. 3 (March,
1959), p. 43.

riddle, is called upon at the beginning of the play to discover who killed Laius. He follows all the clues and finally discovers that he himself is guilty of slaying the Theban king. This is the basis of Francis Fergusson's carefully reasoned interpretation of the play's action in his admirable *The Idea of a Theatre*. I believe it is also the underlying assumption of W. H. Auden's fascinating essay on the detective story, "The Guilty Vicarage," in which he shows that Greek tragedy and the modern detective story share many important common characteristics. Unfortunately, however, as attractive as these interpretations are, Sophocles' text makes it very clear that the question of "Who killed Laius?" is not really the issue at all; it is a red herring, for in actuality we never know for sure who *did* kill Laius. There is the generally accepted account of Laius' death, which has a band of robbers—"almost an army"—kill Laius and his small company, with only one man escaping, who then returns to Thebes to tell the story. Then there is a rumored story that Laius was killed by some travelers with no one escaping. Tiresias is brought in and accuses Oedipus, but as Oedipus rightly asks Creon: "If I was guilty, why did not Tiresias accuse me then? He must have known, for he is wise." Creon can only answer: "I do not know," and the matter is dropped. There is Jocasta's version, which substantiates the public version of the story. Finally, there is Oedipus' own description of the man he killed at the place where the three roads meet, which makes it clear that he was all alone. In good courtroom fashion all of these accounts are brought into question in the following dialogue:

Oedipus
> You said he told you robbers murdered Laius. If he still says "robbers" and not "a robber," I am innocent. One cannot be taken for many. But if he says a murderer alone, the guilt comes to rest on me.

Jocasta
> But we all heard him say "robbers"; that is certain. He cannot unsay it. I am not alone, for the whole city heard.

The investigation never goes beyond this point. To be sure, the Shepherd who is to unravel it all is called, but by the time he comes, the question of "Who killed Laius?" is no longer important and he is never asked. Whether Oedipus killed Laius is never unequivocally determined, and the fact that it is not is not really important to the meaning of the play. With the arrival of the messenger from Corinth the action moves—although it has been going there from the beginning—to the question of Oedipus' identity.

Rather than reading the play as a detective story, I agree with Professor Lattimore, who has shown in his *The Poetry of Greek Tragedy* that the play's action is based upon the general pattern of the lost one found, that *Oedipus the King* is essentially a foundling story. Beginning with Moses, Cyrus, and Romulus, right up to Earnest-Jack Worthing, the foundling story has always been a success story and therefore is usually the plot of a comedy whenever it is employed in the theatre. This is the basis of Mr. Lattimore's interpretation, and he contends that the tension and effectiveness of the play resides in the irony achieved by mounting a tragedy on an essentially comic scheme. With this I disagree! There is no ironic inversion here, for all the way to the end the play *is* a success story. Like the other foundling tales, the action of *Oedipus the King* is a quest—either by discovery or deeds—for identity. Usually the success of this achievement is the cause for joy and celebration ("Our Perdita is found!"), but in *Oedipus the King* the focus is on the disaster of identity. Oedipus succeeds! He finds and he is found. But whenever a man discovers his identity—who he really is as distinct from what others (his parents, siblings, friends, colleagues, and even his enemies) believe or desire him to be—he becomes conscious for the first time of his own unique and individual struggle with necessity. It is the individual's sense of his own identity that transforms Man's Fate into a man's fate. The tragic view of life insists that the assertion of identity—"I am Jesus, the King of the Jews!", "I am Hamlet, the Dane!"—is inextricably bound to suffering and death, the cross and the grave. There is glory in the discovery of self, but it has a price, and great tragedy has always affirmed this ambiguity.

This central ambiguity of tragic action is expressed in *Oedipus the King* by the interweaving lines of the plot, by the conflicts within and between the characters, and in the image patterns of the poetry, especially the play's central image—Mount Cithaeron. It will be remembered that the foundling is always the child of the wilderness, and in Greece the wilderness is in the mountains, and particularly the wild, barren slopes of Mount Cithaeron. Cithaeron, as Jane Harrison has shown in *Themis*, was the home of all foundlings, especially divinely protected heroes, demigods, and even such gods as Dionysus and Zeus. Most critics, Lattimore's being the notable exception, overlook the importance of Mount Cithaeron in the play and yet it is always there towering above the imaginative world of the play as it does, in fact, range above the city of Thebes. In addition to its continual presence in the imagery of the choral odes, it is also the key image in Oedipus' discovery of his identity. When he returns to the stage after tearing out his eyes, he cries out against his fate, shouting: "Cithaeron, why did you let me live? Why / Did you not kill me as I lay there?" and shortly before he leaves the stage for the last time, humbled and having accepted his fate, he calls up the image of the mountain:

> Let me
> Have no home but the mountains, where the hill
> They call Cithaeron, my Cithaeron, stands.
> There my mother and my father, while
> They lived, decreed I should have my grave.
> My death will be a gift from them, for they
> Have destroyed me. . . .

What is the significance of the recurring metaphor of Cithaeron? What is involved in this return to the mountain, the mountain of Oedipus' infancy? Part of an answer can be found in the second choral stasimon. This is one of the most remarkable passages in the play and yet it is often cut in production, and Yeats saw fit to reduce its fifty lines to fifteen in his "more poetic" rendering of the text. But both structurally and thematically it is absolutely essential to an understanding of the play's meaning. Com-

ing as it does right after Oedipus' decision to call the
Shepherd who is to decide once and for all who killed
Laius, it serves as a commentary on the ultimate futility
of those investigations of the intellect which would fathom
the will of the gods and solve the riddles of existence. But
it is also the overture to that movement of the play which
concerns itself with Oedipus' search for his own identity.
In linking the quest for Laius' killer with the larger question of existential identity, this choral passage is both a
judgment and a foreshadowing. The first 38 lines are
particularly significant and worth recalling here:

Chorus
    All actions must beware of the powers beyond us,
        and each word
    Must speak our fear of heaven. I pray
    That I may live every hour in obedience.
    The laws that hold us in subjection
    Have always stood beyond our reach, conceived
    In the high air of heaven. Olympus
    Was their sire, and no woman on earth
    Gave them life. They are laws
    That will never be lured to sleep in the
        arms of oblivion,
    And in their strength heaven is great and
        cannot grow old.
    Yet man desires to be more than man, to rule
    His world for himself.
    This desire, blown to immensity
    On the rich empty food of its ambition,
    Out of place, out of time,
    Clambers to the crown of the rock, and stands there,
    Tottering; then comes the steepling plunge
        down to earth,
    To the earth where we are caged and mastered.
    But this desire may work for good
    When it fights to save a country, and I pray
    That heaven will not weaken it then.
    For then it comes like a god to be our warrior
    And we shall never turn it back.

Justice holds the balance of all things,
And we must fear her.
Do not despise the frontiers in which we must live,
Do not cross them, do not talk of them,
But bow before the places where the gods are throned.
Time will come with cruel vengeance on the man
Who disobeys; that is the punishment
For those who are proud and are more than men—
They are humbled.
If a man grows rich in defiance of this law,
If his actions trespass on a world that he should fear,
If he reaches after mysteries that no man should
    know,
No prayer can plead for him when the sword of
    heaven is raised.
If he were to glory in success
All worship would fall dumb.

In effect, the passage says: "Woe to the climbers of mountains! And yet, where would we be without them!" Man's need to overreach himself, to "despise the frontiers in which we must live," to be a hero, is an essential part of human nature; but all attempts to transcend the limits of being human are inevitably doomed to disaster. Most men know they are incapable of reaching "after mysteries that no man should know," but they nonetheless need and admire those heroes who would dare so audaciously to do so. From the time of Hesiod's *Works and Days,* the mountain climb was the symbol in Greek literature of the hero's impossible quest for perfect *aretē,* that ultimate achievement of mind and spirit which made man like unto gods. To achieve *aretē* requires a tremendous act of will; it is an achievement that only a person with a strong sense of his own identity is capable of attempting and, therefore, it inevitably separates him from the rest of humankind. It is also a demonic quest for it ultimately must transcend the limits of rationality. Oedipus, although unaware of it, has such a demon within him. He finally discovers it, and in his discovery we witness the tragedy of intellectuality.

Our most distinguishing characteristic as human beings

is our self-criticizing intelligence. It is the source of our greatness, but it is also the cause of our most profound grief. It creates the occasions for tragedy in one of two ways: either when our reflective thought challenges the authenticity of our impulses, or when our impulses rebel against those threats to their fulfillment which our reason would erect to maintain itself. Nietzsche described this as the conflict between the Dionysian and the Apollonion, but whether we describe this conflict as one between freedom and domination, Eros and Thanatos, autonomy and constraint, gratification and repression, or genuine progress and eternal return, it makes little difference for it is from the conflict of these two natures in each of us that the tragic experience emerges.

The ambiguity of all tragedy, and this is especially true of *Oedipus the King,* consists of the fact that our doomed need to die is the only means of regaining the spontaneity that life loses under the alienating, repressive systems created by the intelligence. This is the curse of Adam! He paid the price of death for an increase in intelligence. His curse dramatizes the connection between death and culture: the same rational process that strengthens man's chances to live also create the conditions that make death inevitable and even attractive. The great tragedies reenact the necessity and the meaninglessness of this death drama; they show man's ultimate and inevitable alienation, but they also reveal that man's rational faculty is the cause of this condition. This is so because intelligence, in the words of Ralph J. Hallman, "invites man to overreach himself; it discovers to man his fragmented, corrupt nature; it imposes duality upon experience and thereby sets up conflicts . . . it is the source of all painful paradox. It creates the notion of universality, of eternality, of permanence. Rationality alone can conceive of deathlessness, and it therefore creates in man the urge to become immortal. It forces man to expand his personal, limited, finite experiences to a cosmic scale. Thus, it makes possible the idea of an ultimately meaningless universe. It is an agent of domination; yet it creates the conditions of freedom. It militates against aggression; yet aggression cannot occur in its absence. It softens our motor experiences and makes for indolence. It saps life of individuality by forcing it into institutional molds; yet when the individual discovers it within himself, he becomes the rebel." Tragedy, in short, shows why heroes are born, but it also depicts the bankruptcy of intelligence as a measure that one must take in a vain effort to escape the final estrangement.

The foundling story is one of the archetypal expressions of this conflict, and, as Jung and Kerenyi have shown, the Oedipus menace exists in the form of the "Eternal Child" within every one of us. Imbedded in the psychic structure of each individual, it expresses itself as the most fundamental urge to become ourselves through the process of losing ourselves in a retreat to the Cithaeron of our childhood. It is thus potentiality for self-realization; it is the act of returning to the primordial condition where lies the secret power capable of unbinding the fetters of a coercive world and of releasing the self into full freedom. Intelligence creates the possibility of such freedom; it dangles before man the chimerical vision of an autonomous existence, and thus taunts him to rebel. But such freedom can never be realized, for no man can fulfill himself apart from an ordered system even though his very nature demands that he try. Perhaps the history of the whole human race can be telescoped into this one tragic contradiction: man demands freedom, but he wills to submit. Only the tragic hero makes a desperately magnanimous effort to achieve spontaneity, only he refuses to compromise. Thus Oedipus is doomed, but not because he had a tragic flaw, but because he refused to accept a ready-made fate. He wanted his own fate—not the gods! His personal fate may be cut short by his doom, but Oedipus insists upon distinguishing his own responsibility by blinding himself. It is the magnificence of his own declaration of responsibility that makes him so heroic. His fate is *his*, and no one else's. And if he has *hamartia*, it is not a sin or a flaw, but the ungovernable tragic ignorance of all men.

"Oedipus," as we all know, means "swelled foot" when translated from the Greek; but *Oida Pous* also means "on the track of knowledge." Oedipus begins in the play as a hero of knowledge. He would climb Mount Olympus, the home of the gods and the place of wisdom; he has solved the riddle of the Sphinx, which can be answered by an abstraction: MAN. But we must always remember that although the risk of the Sphinx is deadly, its challenge is to the intellect alone. In answering the Sphinx man may be right or wrong, but his answer is rational. But the quest for identity is not a rational undertaking, and here our intelligence fails us. Man's intelligence cannot solve, cover, foresee, or account for all that happens to us. Experience always makes a fool of the mind, for the answer to the question "Who am I?" is an experiential answer and is therefore always unique. Harold Rosenberg in writing about *Oedipus the King* in his fascinating essay "Notes on Identity," said: "The assumption of tragedy is that in actual existence it is impossible to win, except by way of the destruction itself—and winning through being destroyed is not a rational risk but a transcendental hypothesis." Oedipus attempts to understand everything—including his own identity—in a rational way. But for all of his determination and intelligence there is a dark, nonsensical element in experience that eludes his comprehension and thereby leads him to his destruction. Life begins for Oedipus, as in a way it does for each of us, on Mount Cithaeron. He would climb Olympus, only to discover that man's fate is that he end on Cithaeron. His glory is in the climb and his doom in the fall that is inevitable.

> Yet man desires to be more than man, to rule
> His world for himself.
>
> . . . .
>
> Out of place, out of time,
> [He] Clambers to the crown of the rock, and stands
> there
> Tottering; then comes the steepling plunge down to
> earth,
> To the earth where we are caged and mastered.

Such are the conflicts of turbulence and if we are to rescue the plays of Sophocles from those dusty repositories where most masterpieces of culture are usually stored, we must find ways to rediscover that tension of struggle which is inevitable when men try vainly but nobly to impose a meaning on their own lives and on the world around them.

 Antigone

Characters   *Antigone*

Ismene

Chorus

Creon

Guard

Haemon

Teiresias

Messenger

Eurydice

Servant

Antigone

My darling sister Ismene, we have had
A fine inheritance from Oedipus.
God has gone through the whole range of sufferings
And piled them all on us,—grief upon grief,
Humiliation upon humiliation.
And now this latest thing that our dictator
Has just decreed . . . you heard of it? Or perhaps
You haven't noticed our enemies at work.

Ismene

No news, either good or bad, has come
To me, Antigone: nothing since the day
We were bereaved of our two brothers. No,
Since the withdrawal of the Argive army
Last night, I've heard nothing about our loved ones
To make me glad or sad.

Antigone

                   I thought as much.
That's why I hauled you out, outside the gate,
So we could have a talk here undisturbed.

Ismene

You've something on your mind. What is it then?

Antigone

Only that our friend Creon has decided
To discriminate between our brothers' corpses.
Eteocles he buried with full honors
To light his way to hell in a blaze of glory.
But poor dear Polyneices,—his remains
Are not allowed a decent burial.
He must be left unmourned, without a grave,
A happy hunting ground for birds
To peck for titbits. This ukase applies
To you,—and me of course. What's more, friend Creon

Is on his way here now to supervise
Its circulation in person. And don't imagine
He isn't serious,—the penalty
For disobedience is to be stoned to death.
So, there you have it. You're of noble blood.
Soon you must show your mettle,—if you've any.

Ismene

Oh my fire-eating sister, what am I
Supposed to do about it, if this is the case?

Antigone

Just think it over—if you'll give a hand.

Ismene

In doing what? What do you have in mind?

Antigone

Just helping me do something for the corpse.

Ismene

You don't intend to bury him? It's forbidden.

Antigone

He is my brother, and yours. My mind's made up.
You please yourself.

Ismene

But Creon has forbidden . . .

Antigone

What Creon says is quite irrelevant.
He is my brother. I will bury him.

Ismene

Oh, god.
Have you forgotten how our father died
Despised and hated? How he turned
Detective to discover his own crimes,
Then stabbed his own eyes out with his own hands?
And then Jocasta, who was both together
His mother and his wife,
Hanged herself with a rope? Next, our two brothers
Became each other's murderers. We are left,
We two. How terrible if we as well
Are executed for disobeying
The lawful orders of the head of state.
Oh please remember,—we are women, aren't we?
We shouldn't take on men. In times of crisis

It is the strongest men who take control.
We must obey their orders, however harsh.
So, while apologizing to the dead,
Regretting that I act under constraint,
I will comply with my superior's orders.
Sticking one's neck out would be merely foolish.

Antigone
Don't think I'm forcing you. In fact, I wouldn't
Have your assistance if you offered it.
You've made your bed; lie on it. I intend
To give my brother burial. I'll be glad
To die in the attempt,—if it's a crime,
Then it's a crime that God commands. I then
Could face my brother as a friend and look
Him in the eyes. Why shouldn't I make sure
I get on with the dead rather than with
The living? There is all eternity
To while away below. And as for you,
By all means be an atheist if you wish.

Ismene
I'm not. I'm simply powerless to act
Against this city's laws.

Antigone
That's your excuse.
Goodbye. I'm going now to make a grave
For our brother, whom I love.

Ismene
Oh, dear.
I'm terribly afraid for you.

Antigone
Don't make a fuss
On my account,—look after your own skin.

Ismene
At least then promise me that you will tell
No one of this; and I'll keep quiet too.

Antigone
For god's sake don't do that,—you're sure to be
Far more unpopular if you keep quiet.
No; blurt it out, please do.

Ismene
You're very cheerful.

Antigone
  That is because I'm helping those I know
  That I should help.
Ismene
                I only hope you can,
  But it's impossible.
Antigone
                Must I refrain
  From trying just because you say I can't?
Ismene
  If it's impossible, you shouldn't try
  At all.
Antigone
        If that's your line, you've earned my hatred
  And that of our dead brother too, by rights.
  Oh, kindly let me go my foolish way,
  And take the consequences. I will suffer
  Nothing worse than death in a good cause.
Ismene
  All right then, off you go. I'm bound to say
  You're being very loyal but very silly.
Chorus
  At last it has dawned, the day that sees
  The force that rode from Argos driven
  Back upon its road again
  With headlong horses on a looser rein.

  Roused by Polyneices to aid his claim,
  Like an eagle screaming,
  With snow-tipped wings and bloody claws
  And mouth agape, it wheeled about our fortress doors.
  But Thebes, a hissing snake, fought back.
  The god of fire could get no grip
  Upon our crown of walls. That bird of prey,
  Its beak balked of our blood, has turned away.

  God hates presumption. When he saw
  Those men in ostentatious force
  And clash of gold advancing,
  He singled out one man all set
  To shout the victory cry upon the parapet,

And flung at him a lightning bolt, to curtail his prancing.

Covered in flame he dropped
Down like an empty balance and drummed the earth;
He who before had breathed
The winds of hate against us. In many a foray and rout,
War, a runaway horse, was hitting out.

Seven enemy kings at seven gates,
Fighting at equal odds,
Left their arms as trophies to Theban gods.

Elsewhere, the hated pair,
Sons of the same mother,
Crossed their swords in combat and killed each other.

But now that Victory has smiled on us,
Let us forget the war, and dance
At every temple all night long. And let
Bacchus be king in Thebes, until the strong earth reels.

Ah, here comes Creon, our ruler,—in haste.
Something new has developed.
He has something afoot . . .
Else why has he summoned us to council?

Creon
Well, friends, our city has passed through
     stormy weather.
But now God has restored an even keel.
Why have I summoned you? Because I know
That you were at all times loyal to Laius.
And afterwards, when Oedipus put things right
Then ruined them again, you showed
Your steadiness throughout his sons' dispute.
Well, now they're dead; and so, by due succession,
The power of the crown passes to me.
You cannot possibly judge a ruler's worth
Until he exercises the power he's got.
I've no time for the man who has full powers
Yet doesn't use them to enact good measures,
But adopts a timid policy of "do nothing."
Those aren't my principles. I'm not the man

To sit quietly by and watch my country
Sliding towards the precipice of ruin.
Nor can I be a friend to my country's foes.
This I believe—and God may witness it—,
Our safety is bound up with that of our country.
    Therefore
All other loyalties are subject to
Our country's interests.
By such measures I'll make this city great;—
Measures like those which I have just enacted
Concerning Oedipus' sons. That Eteocles
Who died while fighting in his country's service,
Is to be buried with ceremonial honors.
But Polyneices,—whose intention was
To fight his way back from exile, burn to the ground
His mother city and the temples of
His family's gods, to slaughter out of hand
And to enslave his fellow citizens . . .
He's not to have a grave or any mourning.
His corpse is to be left, a grim warning,
Pecked at by birds and worried by the dogs.
That is my policy. A malefactor mustn't
Have the same treatment as the loyal man.
I intend to see our country's friends rewarded
When they are dead, as well as while they live.

Chorus
We understand the attitude you take
Towards these men. It's true your word is law,
And you can legislate for living and dead. . . .

Creon
What do you think then of this new enactment?

Chorus
If I were younger, I might criticize. . . .

Creon
No turning back. The guard is set on the corpse.

Chorus
What are the penalties for disobeying?

Creon
The penalty is death. As simple as that.

Chorus
That ought to stop them. Who'd be such a fool?

Creon
You'd be surprised. Men led astray by hopes
Of gain will risk even their lives for money.

Guard
Sir, here I am. I can't pretend I'm puffed
From running here with all possible speed.
I kept changing my mind on the way.
One moment I was thinking, "What's the hurry?
You're bound to catch it when you get there." Then,
"What are you dithering for? You'll get it hot
And strong if Creon finds out from someone else."
Torn by these doubts I seem to have taken my time.
So what should be a short journey has become
A long one. Anyway I have arrived.
And now I'm going to tell you what I came
To tell you, even if you've heard it. See,
I've made up my mind to expect the worst.
We can't avoid what's coming to us, can we?

Creon
Well then, what puts you in such deep despair?

Guard
First I must make a statement—about myself.
I didn't do it, and didn't see who did it.
So I'm quite in the clear, you understand.

Creon
For God's sake tell me what it is, and then
Clear off.

Guard
              All right, all right. It amounts to this.
Somebody's buried the body, thrown earth on it,
And done the necessary purifications.

Creon
Someone has been a stupid fool. Who was it?

Guard
Dunno. There were no spade marks in the earth.
The ground was hard and dry, and yet there was
No sign of the intruder.
See, when the man who had the first day-watch
Told us about it, we had the shock of our lives.
The corpse had not been buried in a grave,
But enough dust was thrown on to avoid

The curse unburied bodies suffer from.
There wasn't even a sign of any dog
That might have come and scuffed the dust upon him.
Then everyone started shouting. Each man blamed
His mate. We damned near came to blows.
Everyone claimed that one of the others had done it,
And tried to prove that he himself was blameless.
To prove their innocence, some said they were
Prepared to pick up red-hot coals or walk
Through fire. While others swore on oath
By a catalogue of gods, they didn't do it
And weren't accomplices in any form.
When our investigations made no progress,
In the end one chap came out with a sobering speech.
We couldn't answer him, though what he said
Was none too pleasant.
He said we mustn't try to hush it up,
But tell you everything. His view prevailed.
Who was to bring the news? We tossed for it.
I was the lucky person. I can tell you,
I don't like being the bearer of bad news.

Chorus

I think I see the hand of God in this,
Bringing about the body's burial.

Creon

Shut up, before I lose my temper.
You may be old, try not to be foolish as well.
How can you say God cares about this corpse?
Do you suppose God feels obliged to him
For coming to burn down His temples and
His statues, in defiance of His laws?
Ever noticed God being kind to evildoers?
No. Certain hostile elements in the city
Who don't like discipline and resent my rule,
Are in on this. They've worked upon the guards
By bribes. There is no human institution
As evil as money. Money ruins nations,
And makes men refugees. Money corrupts
The best of men into depravity.
The people who have done this thing for money
Will get what's coming to them. Listen here,

I swear to you by God who is my judge,
That if you and your friends do not divulge
The name of him who did the burying,
One hell won't be enough for you. You'll all
Be hanged up and flogged until you tell.
That ought to teach you to be more selective
About what you get your money from.

Guard

Am I dismissed?
Or may I speak?

Creon

I thought I made it plain
I couldn't stand your talk.

Guard

Where does it hurt you,—
Your ears, or in your mind?

Creon

What do you mean?
What does it matter where you give me pain?

Guard

The guilty party suffers most inside.
But my offence is only at ear level.

Creon

Listen, soldier. You talk too much.

Guard

You might be right, but I am not your culprit.

Creon

I think you are, and that you did it for money.

Guard

You're wrong! I tell you your suspicions are wrong.

Creon

Suspicion he calls it! Look here, if someone here
Doesn't tell me who the culprits are, you'll find
That ill-gotten gains are not without their drawbacks.

Guard

Good luck to you, I hope you find the guy.
In any case I won't be in a hurry
To come back here again. I thank my stars
That I have saved my skin. I didn't expect to.

Chorus

Many amazing things exist, and the most amazing is man.

He's the one, when the gale-force winds
Blow and the big waves
Tower and topple on every side,
Cruises over the deep on the gray tide.

He's the one that to and fro
Over the clods year after year
Wends with his horses and ploughing gear,
Works to his will the untiring Earth, the greatest of gods.

He traps the nitwit birds, and the wild
Beasts in their herds. The ocean's myriad clan
In woven nets he catches,—ingenious man.

He has devised himself shelter against
The rigors of frost and the pelting weather.
Speech and science he's taught himself,
And the city's political arts for living together.

For incurable diseases he has found a cure
By his inventiveness, defying
Every eventuality there can be,—except dying.

But the most brilliant gifts
Can be misapplied.
On his moral road
Man swerves from side to side.

God and the government ordain
Just laws; the citizen
Who rules his life by them
Is worthy of acclaim.

But he that presumes
To set the law at naught
Is like a stateless person,
Outlawed, beyond the pale.

With such a man I'd have
No dealings whatsoever.

In public and in private
He'd get the cold shoulder.

What's this? What on earth?
My god. Can it be? Yes, Antigone.
Your father before, now you!
Is it so, you were caught disobeying the law?
How could you have been so stupid?

Guard

Here she is. She is the one,—the one who did it.
We caught her in the act. Where's Creon gone?

Chorus

There, by good luck he's coming out right now.

Creon

Soon as I leave the house, some trouble starts.
What's happening?

Guard

Well, well, I never thought
That I'd be coming back here again so soon,
Considering how you swore at me just now.
But here I am, in spite of what I said.
I'm bringing in this girl. I caught her tending
The grave. I caught her, no one else. And so
I hand her over to you to stand her trial.
And now, if you don't mind, I'm getting out of here.

Creon

Give me full details, with the circumstances.

Guard

This girl was burying him. As simple as that.

Creon

I trust you understand what you are saying.

Guard

I saw her burying the corpse you said
Was not allowed to be buried. Clear enough?

Creon

Tell me precisely how you saw and caught her.

Guard

It was like this. When we got back,
With your threats still smarting in our ears,
We swept all the dust from off the corpse,
And laid the mouldering thing completely bare.

Then we went and sat on the high ground to windward,
To avoid the smell. And everyone gave hell
To the man who was on duty, to keep him up
To scratch. He watched till midday, when the sun
Is hottest. Suddenly a squall came on,—
Whirlwind with a thunderstorm; it ripped
The leaves from every tree in all the plain.
The air was full of it; we had to keep
Our eyes tight shut against the wrath of heaven.
At last, when all was over, there we see
The girl,—crying like a bird that finds
Its nest empty of chicks,—her having seen
The corpse uncovered. Then she started cursing
Whoever did it. Next she goes and fetches
Dust in her hands; and from a jug she pours
A set of three libations on the corpse.
When we saw that, of course we jumped straight up
And grabbed the girl. She took it very calmly.
We charged her with this crime and the previous one,
And she admitted them. So I'm half-glad,
Half-sorry. Glad that I am out of danger,
But sorry someone that I like's in trouble.
However, main thing is that I'm all right.

Creon

You, with your eyes fixed on the ground.
Do you admit the charges or deny them?

Antigone

I don't deny the charges. I admit them.

Creon

[*To* GUARD] All right, get out! Consider yourself lucky
To be absolved of guilt.
[*To* ANTIGONE] Now tell me, briefly,—I don't want a speech.
You knew about my edict which forbade this?

Antigone

Of course I knew. You made it plain enough.

Creon

You took it on yourself to disobey?

Antigone

Sorry, who made this edict? Was it God?
Isn't a man's right to burial decreed

By divine justice? I don't consider your
Pronouncements so important that they can
Just . . . overrule the unwritten laws of heaven.
You are a man, remember.
These divine laws are not just temporary measures.
They stand for ever. I would have to face
Them when I died. And I will die, without
Your troubling to arrange it. So, what matter
If I must die before my time? I'd welcome
An early death, living as I do now.
What I can't stand is passively submitting
To my own brother's body being unburied.
I dare say you think I'm being silly.
Perhaps you're not so very wise yourself.

Chorus
She's difficult, just like her father was.
She doesn't realize when to give in.

Creon
I know these rigid temperaments. They're the first
To break. The hardest tempered steel
Will shatter at a blow. The highest-mettled
Horses are broken in with a small bit.
That's what is needed, discipline. This girl
Knew damned well she was kicking over the traces,
Breaking the law. And now when she has done it,
She boasts about it, positively gloats.
If she gets away with this behavior,
Call me a woman and call her a man.
I don't care if she is my sister's daughter.
I don't care if she's closer to me than all
My family. She and her sister won't get off.
I'll execute them.   Oh, yes, her as well.
She's in it too. Go and get her. She's inside.
I saw her in there muttering, half-crazy.
It is her conscience. She can't hide her guilt.
At least she doesn't try to justify it.

Antigone
Will my death be enough? Do you want more?

Creon
No, that will do, as far as I'm concerned.

Antigone
>Then why not do it now? Our wills conflict
>Head on. No chance of reconciliation.
>I can't think of a finer reason for dying,—
>Guilty of having buried my own brother.
>These men are on my side. But they daren't say so.

Creon
>That's where you're wrong. You're quite alone in this.

Antigone
>They're on my side. They're forced to cringe to you.

Creon
>These men obey. But you and you alone
>Decided to disobey. Aren't you ashamed?

Antigone
>Ashamed? Ashamed of what? Ashamed of being
>Loyal to my own family, my own brother?

Creon
>Eteocles was also your own brother.

Antigone
>Indeed he was. Of course he was my brother.

Creon
>Then why were you so disloyal to him?

Antigone
>If he were living now, he'd back me up.

Creon
>For treating his brother no differently from him!

Antigone
>It was his brother that died, not just some servant.

Creon
>Died while commanding an invading force!
>But Eteocles died fighting for his country.

Antigone
>That doesn't affect the laws of burial.

Creon
>You can't treat friend and enemy the same.

Antigone
>Who knows what the rules are among the dead?

Creon
>Your enemy doesn't become your friend by dying.

Antigone
>If we must have these groupings, let me say

I'll join anyone in loving, but not in hating.

Creon

All right then, die, and love them both in hell.
I'm not here to be shoved around by a woman.

Chorus

Oh, look, by the gate, here's Ismene.
She's crying because of her sister.
What a shame this heavy cloud of grief
Should spoil her attractive appearance.

Creon

And now for you. You who've being skulking quiet,
Injecting your slow poison like a viper.
Imagine my not noticing,—I've been rearing
Two furies in my house, ready to bite
The hand that fed them. Just you tell me now—
Will you confess you were party to this burial,
Or will you swear you had no knowledge of it?

Ismene

I did it, if she did it. I'm involved.
I'm in with her and bear my share of blame.

Antigone

That's quite unjustified. You didn't want
To help me, and I didn't let you join me.

Ismene

You are in trouble. May I then not make
Myself your comrade in adversity?

Antigone

The dead know who it was that did the deed.
You took no action. Your speeches don't impress me.

Ismene

How can you, being my sister, deny my wish
To die with you for Polyneices' sake?

Antigone

Don't go and die as well as me, and don't
Lay claim to what you haven't done. I'm going
To die. One death's enough.

Ismene

Will life be worth
Living to me left all alone without you?

Antigone

May I suggest an object of affection?

Creon. He is your uncle, after all.
Ismene
Why do you try to hurt me? What's the point?
Antigone
I may make fun of you, but I feel this deeply.
Ismene
I only want to know how I can help you.
Antigone
Well, save yourself then. I don't grudge you that.
Ismene
I don't want that. I want to die with you.
Antigone
You chose to live; I chose to die, remember?
Ismene
I didn't express my innermost convictions.
Antigone
You sounded pretty convinced at the time.
Ismene
I still maintain that we two share the guilt.
Antigone
Don't worry. You won't die. But I've already
Sacrificed my life to help the dead.
Creon
These girls! One of them's been mad all her life.
And now the other one's gone crazy too.
Ismene
But, sir, however sensible one is,
Adversity is bound to affect one's judgment.
Creon
Well, it has yours! You join this criminal,
And identify yourself with her misdeeds.
Ismene
There is no life left for me without her.
Creon
Forget about her. She's as good as dead.
Ismene
So you would execute your own son's bride?
Creon
Plenty of other women in the world.
Ismene
But they were so well-suited to each other.

Creon
I won't have my son marrying a bitch.

Antigone
Poor Haemon! See how much your father cares.

Creon
Oh, go to hell,—you and your marriage with you.

Ismene
You really intend to take her from your son?

Creon
I won't stop the marriage. Death will stop it.

Ismene
There's no way out? It is fixed that she dies?

Creon
Of course it's fixed. Stop wasting time.
You! Servants, take her in. It's very important
To keep women strictly disciplined.
That's the deterrent. Even the bravest people
Will retreat quickly when they see death loom up.

Chorus
Happy the man whose life is uneventful.
For once a family is cursed by God,
Disasters come like earthquake tremors, worse
With each succeeding generation.

It's like when the sea is running rough
Under stormy winds from Thrace.
The black ooze is stirred up from the seabed,
And louder and louder the waves crash on shore.

Look now at the last sunlight that sustains
The one surviving root of Oedipus' tree,—
The sword of death is drawn to hack it down.

And all through nothing more than intemperate
    language.
All through nothing more than hasty temper.

What power on earth can resist
Your strength, O God? You stand supreme,
Untouched by sleep that makes all else feel old,
Untired by the passing years that wear all else away.

I know one rule that has stood,
And will stand, forever.
That nothing in our life can be exempt
From the universal forces that make for ruin.

Hope, that tramps all roads, may help at times.
More often, it deludes weak-minded men.
They never notice, till they feel the fire.

It is a wise saying, that
When God is set against you,
You welcome the path to ruin,—but not for long.

Here comes Haemon, your youngest son.
I expect he's grieved about his bride,
And this sudden bar to his marriage.

Creon

There's one way of finding out for certain.
My son, you've heard about this public decree.
Have you come here in a spirit of indignation
About your bride, or are you going to be
Loyal to me whatever I'm involved in?

Haemon

I am your son. So while your policies
Are just, you have my full obedience.
I certainly wouldn't consider any marriage
As important as the right leadership by you.

Creon

Good, good. Your heart is in the right place. Nothing
Should come before your loyalty to your father.
Why else do fathers pray for well-behaved sons?
They do things together. Work together against
Their common enemy. Vie with each
Other in being good friends to their friends.
As for the man who brings up useless sons,
He's got himself a load of trouble,—all
His enemies laugh at them, a bad team.
Never get carried away by a woman, son.
Sex isn't everything. If she's a bitch,
You'll feel a coldness as she lies beside you.

Can there be anything worse than giving your love
To a bitch that doesn't deserve it? No, reject her,
And let her go and find a husband in hell.
Now that I've caught her flagrantly disobeying
When everybody else has toed the line,
The eyes of the nation are on me. I must stay
True to my principles. I must execute her.
I don't give a damn for all her talk
About family ties. If I allow
My own relations to get out of control,
That gives the cue to everybody else.
People who are loyal members of their families
Will be good citizens too. But if a person
Sets himself up above the law and tries
To tell his rulers what they ought to do,—
You can't expect me to approve of that.
Once a man has authority, he must be obeyed,—
In big things and in small, in every act
Whether just or not so just. I tell you this,
The well-disciplined man is good
At giving orders and at taking them too.
In war, in a crisis, he's the sort of man
You like to have beside you. On the other hand,
There's nothing so disastrous as anarchy.
Anarchy means an ill-disciplined army,
A rabble that will break into a panic rout.
What follows? Plundered cities, homeless people.
A disciplined army loses few men;
Discipline pulls them through to victory.
We can't go about kowtowing to women.
If I must lose my throne, let it be a man
That takes it from me. I can't have people saying
My will has been defeated by a woman.

Chorus

I think your observations very just,
In general . . . though perhaps I'm old and silly.

Haemon

Father, don't you agree,—
Of all God's gifts good sense is far the best.
I'm sure I'd be the last person to deny
That what you said is true. Yet there may be

A lot of justice in the opposite view.
I've one advantage over you,—I know
Before you what the people think about you,
Especially criticism. You're so held in awe
That people dare not say things to your face.
But I am able to hear their secret talk.
The people feel very sorry for Antigone.
They say it isn't equitable she must die
A horrible death for such a noble action.
They say that she in fact deserves especial
Honor for refusing to allow
The body of her brother to be left
Unburied for dogs and birds to pull to pieces.
That is their secret opinion, and it's gaining ground.
Of course I want your rule to be a success.
There's nothing more important to me than that.
Such feeling is mutual, between father and son,—
One's glad to see the other doing well.
Don't be too single-minded, then. Don't think
You have a complete monopoly of the truth.
Isn't it true that people who refuse
To see any other point of view but theirs
Often get shown up and discredited?
However acute one is, there's no disgrace
In being able to learn, being flexible.
In winter, when the streams turn into torrents,
You can see the trees that try to resist the water
Get rooted out and killed. But those that bend
A little, manage to survive the flood.
In a gale at sea if you cram on full sail,
You'll soon have the waves breaking aboard
And bowling over all the furniture.
Why not relax and change your mind for once?
Perhaps at my age I should not express
An opinion, but I would like to say this:—
Not everyone can be right on every issue,
But the next best thing is to take notice of
And learn from the judicious thoughts of others.

Chorus

Yes, everyone can learn. You, sir, can learn
From him,—and he of course from you. There's much

Of substance in the arguments on both sides.

Creon
Am I to stand here and be lectured to
By a kid? A man of my experience!

Haemon
I'm not suggesting anything illegal.
I may be young, but judge me by the facts.

Creon
The facts are you're encouraging my detractors.

Haemon
I'm not encouraging anything that's wrong.

Creon
You seem to have caught Antigone's disease.

Haemon
The people of Thebes don't call it a disease.

Creon
Must I ask their permission for everything?

Haemon
You're talking like an adolescent now.

Creon
Am I the king of Thebes, or am I not?

Haemon
It takes more than one person to make a nation.

Creon
But a nation is personified in its ruler.

Haemon
In that case Thebes has no population.

Creon
I take it you are siding with this woman.

Haemon
It is your interests I have at heart.

Creon
You show it by arguing against me?

Haemon
Because I think you're making a mistake.

Creon
Must I let my authority be undermined?

Haemon
Yes, rather your authority than God's.

Creon
What character! Subservient to a woman.

Haemon
Subservient to what I think is right.
Creon
You've done nothing but back Antigone up.
Haemon
Not only her, but God, and you as well.
Creon
Don't try to butter me up, you lady's man.
Haemon
You like to talk, but you're not prepared to listen.
Creon
This woman will not live to marry you.
Haemon
Then she won't be the only one to die.
Creon
Oh, oh. Threats is it now? You've got a nerve.
Haemon
I'm trying to show you that you're being perverse.
Creon
You will regret you tried to schoolmaster me.
Haemon
If you weren't my father, I'd say you were deranged.
Creon
What's that? I've had enough of your abuse.
By heaven, I swear I'll make you suffer for it.
Take that hellcat away. You'll watch her die.
Ha, she will die in front of her bridegroom's nose.
Haemon
I won't give you that satisfaction.
I won't be around when she dies.
You must find other friends to condone your madness.
You will never set eyes on me again.
Chorus
He's rushed off in a really furious temper.
He's young,—I fear he may do something rash.
Creon
Let him.
Who does he think he is, God almighty?
In any case, he won't save these girls from death.
Chorus
You don't mean to execute them both?

Creon
No, no. You're right. Not her that wasn't involved.

Chorus
What sort of execution do you intend?

Creon
I'll take her to a deserted spot
And bury her alive in a trench.
She'll have enough food to avoid the curse,—
The people mustn't suffer because of her.
There she can pray to the god she likes so much,—
The god of death. Perhaps he'll save her life.
Either that, or she'll find out too late
That corpses are more trouble than they're worth.

Chorus
What is it that nestles in
The soft cheeks of a girl,
And pervades the deep sea and the teeming earth?
And persecutes god and man, a force
Irresistible? We call it Love.

A man possessed by Love loses control.
Love drives the law-abiding into crime;
And sets a family against itself.

So here a lovely girl's appealing glance
Has prevailed, and destroyed the bonds of blood.
For Love makes mock of time-honored laws
Ordaining loyalty from son to father.

And grief also is irresistible.
The tears come to my eyes,—I cannot stop them;
Seeing Antigone go to such a bed,
The bed that puts all mortal things to sleep.

Antigone
Take a good look. With life still strong in me,
I'm going on my last journey, seeing
For the last time the bright rays of the sun.
Unmarried, never having heard my wedding song,
Death takes me to the dark riverbanks to be his bride.

Chorus
You have one glorious consolation.

By your own choice you go down to death
Alive, not wasted by disease,
Nor hacked by instruments of war.

Antigone

I shall go to sleep like Niobe.
I know her story well. On Mount Sipylus
The rock grew, like ivy, round her and weighed
    her down.
And now the rain and snow
Make tears that run across her stony face.

Chorus

There's no comparison. For she was born
Of divine parentage. You would be lucky
To share the fate of mythical heroines.

Antigone

Are you getting at me? Wait till I'm dead.
I'm going to die,—do I merit no respect?
O my city, O my friends, rich householders,
O River Dirce, with the sacred grove
Of Thebes the Charioteer, I call you all
To witness that I die with nobody
To shed a tear for me, the victim
Of an unjust law. Who'd like to go with me
To an eerie heap of stones, a tomb that is no tomb,
A no-man's-land between the living and the dead?

Chorus

You tried to do the right thing by your brother.
You stepped boldly toward the altar of Justice;
But somehow stumbled. I fear you must suffer
For your father's sins.

Antigone

Don't speak of it again. It's only too well known,—
My father's fate. To think how much
Our family was admired, in generations past.
Then came successive strokes of doom. My mother's
Marriage to her son, the union
From which I came, to end like this.
My brother, dishonored, drags me down with him.
And so I go to join my stricken family in hell.

Chorus

We respect what you did for your brother.

But there's no question that the orders
Of those in authority must be obeyed.
You were self-willed. That has been your undoing.

Antigone

I see I have no friends to say goodbye.
No friends, no tears for me, no marriage to look back on.
Never again to see the face of the sun.

Creon

If I don't stop this blubbering, we'll be here
All night. Stop wasting time. Take her away.
As my instructions state, you are to place
Her in the vaulted trench, and brick it in.
It's up to her then,—either live or die.
My hands are clean in this. I've merely
Deprived her of all contact with the living.

Antigone

This stone dugout, half tomb, half bridal chamber,
Will house me now for good. By this road
I go below to Queen Persephone's kingdom,
To see again so many of my family.
As I am the latest recruit, so is my fate
By far the cruelest. And I've not used
My life's full span.
At least I can look forward to a warm
Welcome from my dear mother and father and
My brother Eteocles. When they were dead,
I washed them and prepared them for the grave
With my own hands, and poured libations over them.
But now, for doing the same to Polyneices,
This is my reward. Because Creon thinks
I have committed an act of brazen defiance.
For this I'm being dragged off by force,
Deprived of my chance to marry and raise children.
I'm to be buried alive, not very pleasant . . .
I just want to ask, what moral law
Have I disobeyed? But what's the point
Of appealing to God? Or asking
Help from my fellow humans? It appears
That virtue is to be repaid by malice.
If that is God's idea of what is right,
Then I apologize; I made a mistake.

But if Creon is wrong, I only hope
He isn't treated any better than me.

Chorus

A hurricane of passionate conviction
Still sweeps her mind.

Creon

What are you all standing about for? Get out! Or else . . .
Hurry, and off with her.

Antigone

Oh, right before me now. Death.

Chorus

If you had any hopes, I should forget them.
Your punishment is fixed. There's no appeal.

Antigone

This is it. The time has come.
For doing what was right,
I'm dragged away to death.
And, Thebes, city where I was born,
And you my friends, the rich people of Thebes,
Will you judge between us?
You might at least look and remember.

Chorus

My poor child, what must be
Must be. Console yourself,
Such things have happened before.

There's nothing that can win the fight
Against the force of destiny;
Not wealth, or military might,
Or city walls, or ships that breast the sea.

Lycurgus, king of Thrace, tried to stop
The bacchanal women and their torchlit orgies.
For his vindictive rage,
He lost his liberty with his temper, locked
By Bacchus in a mountain cave
To let his anger simmer down.

In Salmydessus on the Euxine Sea,
The two sons of Phineus lost their eyes.

In their stepmother's hand, a pointed shuttle . . .
And their blood on her nails cried out for vengeance.

But their mother was jailed in a cavern
Under a steep mountain far away.
She was Cleopatra, the North-Wind's daughter.
A god's daughter, but fate weighed her down.

[*Enter* TEIRESIAS, *led by a boy.*

Teiresias
Councillors of Thebes, I have come,—
A man with four eyes, half of them blind.

Creon
It's old Teiresias. What's up, old fellow?

Teiresias
Listen, and I will tell you. I'm no liar . . .

Creon
I've never suggested that. Quite the reverse.

Teiresias
By doing so, you were able to save Thebes.

Creon
True, I have found what you have said most useful.

Teiresias
Listen to me. You're on the razor's edge.

Creon
What's wrong? The way you talk gives me a turn.

Teiresias
You may think nothing's wrong. But my skill
Says differently.
I went to my accustomed place
Of augury, where there's a wide view of
The sky, to observe the birds. There I heard
An unprecedented din of birds, barbarous,
Confused, as though some madness stung them into
Screaming. I heard them fighting with their claws;
The noise was unmistakable, their wings
Whirring . . . And I felt fear. Immediately
I tried the burnt sacrifices, but
They gave no flame. Only a damp vapor
Smoldered and spat. The gall burst in the fire,
Exposing the thighbones bare of fat.
The boy saw all this and told it me.

Thus I interpret. These sighs portend evil
For Thebes; and the trouble stems from your policy.
Why? Because our altars are polluted
By flesh brought by dogs and birds, pickings
From Polyneices' corpse. Small wonder that
The gods won't accept our sacrifices.
My son, I ask you to consider well
What you are doing. We all make mistakes.
The wise man, having made an error of judgment,
Will seek a remedy, not keep grinding on.
Obstinacy isn't far removed from folly.
The man is dead. No need to persecute him.
You can give way, with good grace, to a corpse.
He has died once, why try to kill him again?
I'm saying this because I wish you well.
A bit of sound advice is always welcome.

Creon

Money! Must everyone set their cap at me
Because of money? Even you augurers
Have formed a corporation to exploit me.
For years now I have been traded about
By your gang in the open market like
A piece of merchandise. All right, rake in
The cash, pile up the wealth of Lydia
And all the gold of India in bribes.
You'll never persuade me to bury that corpse.
Not even if the eagles of Zeus decide
To carry off its flesh in their claws
And place it right on their master's throne.
I refuse for the simple reason that
It's quite impossible for any man
To throw pollution on the gods. They are
Inviolate. But certain gifted men
That I could mention do not seem to mind
A little sharp practice, in the matter
Of telling a lie or two, strictly for cash.

Teiresias

Well!
Can there exist a man who doesn't know . . .

Creon

Watch out, here comes another resounding cliché!

Teiresias
… Good sense is a man's most precious attribute?

Creon
"And bad judgment is a great encumbrance"?

Teiresias
It's an encumbrance you have plenty of.

Creon
… No.
You started it, but I won't insult a "seer."

Teiresias
You've done that already,—accused me of lying.

Creon
The whole lot of you seers are on the make.

Teiresias
Kings also have been known to make their pile.

Creon
Are you implying some reflection on me?

Teiresias
You wouldn't be king now, but for me.

Creon
You're good at your job. But you've gone crooked.

Teiresias
Much more of this, and you'll make me reveal …

Creon
Reveal away. But straight, and not for bribes.

Teiresias
You'll wish you had bribed me not to speak.

Creon
Don't try to pull the wool over my eyes.

Teiresias
The sun won't run its course for many days
Before you have to repay a corpse of your own,
One of your own children as recompense.
One body that belongs to this world
You have locked up in a tomb. Another body
That rightly should be in the underworld
You have forcibly retained here on earth.
Because of this, the Furies have been waiting
To pay you back in your own coin. And so
It won't be long before your house is full
Of grief; I can see men and women crying.

Make up your own mind whether I've been bribed
To say this. Yes, it hurts. But you provoked me.
My boy, take me home. I'm not so young,—
I dare not be around when he explodes.
I only hope he learns from this to show
A little sense and keep a civil tongue.

Chorus

That is a horrible prophecy.
I'm bound to say I've never known him wrong
In any of his predictions.

Creon

                 Yes, I know,
I know. I can't pretend that I'm not worried.
The consequences of giving in are terrible.
But if I hold out, I court disaster.

Chorus

The right decision now is vitally important.

Creon

What should I do then? Tell me what to do.

Chorus

You'll have to go and set Antigone free,
And give the exposed corpse a burial.

Creon

Is that your real opinion? To give in?

Chorus

And waste no time about it, for the wrath
Of God will not be slow to catch you up.

Creon

Can't fight against what's destined. It is hard,
But I'll change my mind. You servants,—
Bring axes, hurry, and come with me. I must
Personally undo what I have done.
I shouldn't have tried being unorthodox.
I'll stick by the established laws in the future.

Chorus

We call on you Bacchus, god of many names,
And god of many places.
You were once a little child
In Thebes here, the darling of your mother's eye.
Your father was Zeus, lord of the thundering sky;
But your mother was Semele, a Theban girl.

Are you among the rich cities
Of Italy? Or presiding
Over the cosmopolitan crowds
That throng the Eleusinian Games?

Perhaps the firebrand lights your face
Between the twin peaks of Mount Parnassus,
Where the Corycian nymphs
Dance by the shores of Castaly.

Perhaps you hear the songs of poets
Where the ivy wreathes the crags
On Nysa, looking over green
Vineyards clustering on the plain.

But this is your home,—the oil-like waters
Of Ismene river, and the fields
Where the dragon's teeth were sown.

This is your mother city, Thebes.
This is the city you honor most.
If ever you heard us before, come to us now.

Our nation is in the grip of a dread disease.
Hasten to help us, speed to doctor our pain
Over the slopes of Parnes hill or over the roaring seas.

Messenger
Citizens of Thebes, who knows how long
Their luck will last? Whether you're up or down,
It's all pure chance. You can't predict what's coming.
Take Creon now. I thought he was doing well,—
The savior of his country, king of Thebes,
And the proud father of a lovely family.
He's lost the lot. Oh, yes, he's wealthy still;
But wealth can't buy you happiness. What's the use
Of money without the means of enjoying it?
His wealth's no more to him than a puff of smoke.
You can't say Creon lives; he's just a walking corpse.

Chorus
About Creon's family, is there bad news then?

Messenger
They're dead. And those that live deserve to die.

Chorus

How did they die? Who's dead? Why can't you tell me?

Messenger

Haemon is dead. Committed suicide.

Chorus

He killed himself? His father didn't do it?

Messenger

Suicide, because Creon had murdered her.

Chorus

Teiresias' prophecy was all too true.

Messenger

That's what has happened. Now it's up to you.

Chorus

Here is Eurydice, Creon's wife, poor woman.
Why is she comng out? Perhaps she's heard . . .

Eurydice

As I was going out, I heard you talking.
I was opening the door when I heard it,
Some more bad news about my children. I fainted,
But my maids held me up. Tell me about it.
I am quite used to suffering.

Messenger

I'll tell you everything, my dear mistress.
I was there, you know. No sense in glossing things over;
You've got to hear it sometime.
I went with my master, your husband, to the place
Where Polyneices' corpse was exposed,
Cruelly torn by dogs. We said prayers
Placating Hecate and Pluto; then we washed
The body to purify it, gathered branches
Of olive, and cremated him or what
Was left of him. We piled him up a mound
Of his mother earth; then went to get
Antigone. While we were on the way,
Somebody heard a sound of crying coming
From the stone chamber. He went up to Creon
And told him of it. Creon hurried on.
As we got near, the sound was all around us,—
Impossible to tell whose it was.
But Creon, in a voice breaking with grief,
Said "Dare I prophesy? These yards of ground

Will prove the bitterest journey of my life.
It's faint, but it's my son's voice. Hurry, men,
Get round the tomb, pull back the stones, and look
Inside. Is it Haemon's voice, or do the gods
Delude me?" At the far end of the tomb
We saw Antigone hanging by the neck
In a noose of linen. He was hugging her
And talking bitterly of their marriage and
His father's action. Creon saw him and
Cried out and ran in shouting "Oh, my son,
What is this? What possessed you? Why are you trying
To kill yourself? Come out now, please, I beg you."
His son made no reply, just looked at him
Savagely with a look of deep contempt.
Then he suddenly drew his sword, evaded Creon,
Held it out, and plunged the blade into his ribs.
He collapsed against Antigone's arms, which were
Still warm, and embraced her. Then his blood
　　　came coughing,
And covered all her white cheeks with scarlet.
So now he lies, one corpse upon another;
And thus their marriage is consummated,—in hell.
It only goes to show good sense is best,
When all this tragedy comes from one rash action.

Chorus
What a strange thing. Eurydice has gone,
Without saying a word.

Messenger
　　　　　　　　It is surprising.
I dare say she's too well-bred to go
Showing her grief in public. I expect
She's gone to have a good cry inside.

Chorus
Perhaps. Noisy grief is a bad thing.
But this extraordinary silence is ominous.

Messenger
You're right. Let's go in then, and find out.
She may have had her mind on something rash.

Chorus
Who's coming? Creon with
The body of his son.

If truth be told, he is
Himself the murderer.

Creon

Wrong! How could I have been so wrong?
And these deaths I caused—you have seen them—
In my own family by my stubbornness.
Oh my son, so young, to die so young,
And all because of me!

Chorus

It's a bit late to find out you were wrong.

Creon

I know that. God has taken his revenge,
Leapt on my head and beaten me
And trampled on the only joy I had.
And all the years that I have labored—wasted.

Servant

My lord, what you see before your eyes,—
It isn't all. You'd better come inside.

Creon

What fresh disaster could I suffer now?

Servant

Your wife, the mother of this corpse, is dead.
Only a moment ago, she stabbed herself.

Creon

Oh death, can I never wash it away?
Why are you destroying me? What
Is your message now? Why stab me again?
My wife dead too?

Servant

See for yourself. They've brought the body out.

Creon

Oh.
Another blow. What else has fate in store?
My wife, my son.

Servant

Stabbed herself by the altar, and so passed on.
But first she bewailed Megareus' death,
Her first son that was, then Haemon's death.
And her last words were curses on your head.

Creon

Now I'm afraid. Why wasn't I killed?

Why didn't somebody kill me, stab me to death?

Servant
Before she died she made a point of planting
The guilt of these two deaths squarely on you.

Creon
How did she die? How did she kill herself?

Servant
I told you. Stabbed herself. Under the heart.
Soon as she heard about her son's death.

Creon
Nobody else to share the blame. Just me . . .
I killed you. I killed you, my dear.
Servants, carry me in, away from all this.
I wish I weren't alive.

Chorus
Try to forget. It is the only way.

Creon
I invite death. Do you only come uninvited?
Come and take me. I cannot bear to live.

Chorus
No time for such thoughts now. You're still in charge.
You've got to see about these corpses, or
We'll all be polluted.

Creon
                    I meant what I said.

Chorus
No use in such prayers. You'll get what's destined.

Creon
Lead me away, a wreck, a useless wreck.
I'll keep out of the way. I killed them both.
Everything has crumbled. I feel
A huge weight on my head.

Chorus
Who wants happiness? The main
Requirement is to be sensible.
This means not rebelling against
God's law, for that is arrogance.
The greater your arrogance, the heavier God's revenge.
And proud men in old age learn to be wise.

—Translated by Michael Townsend

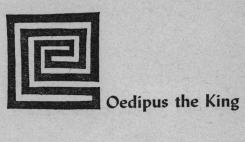

Oedipus the King

Characters   *Oedipus, King of Thebes*

Priest

Creon, Brother of Jocasta

Teiresias, an old blind prophet

Jocasta, wife of Oedipus

Messenger

Shepherd

Servant

In front of the palace of OEDIPUS *at Thebes. Near the altar
stands the* PRIEST *with a large crowd of supplicants.*
[*Enter* OEDIPUS.

Oedipus

My children, why do you crowd and wait at my altars?
Olive branches . . . and wreathes of sacred flowers—
Why do you bring these, my people of Thebes?
    Your streets
Are heavy with incense, solemn with prayers for healing,
And when I heard your voices, I would not let
My messengers tell me what you said. I came
To be your messenger myself, Oedipus, whose name
Is greatest known and greatest feared.

[*To* PRIEST] Will you tell me, then? You have dignity
    enough
To speak for them all—is it fear that makes you kneel
Before me, or do you need my help? I am ready,
Whatever you ask will be done . . . Come, I am not cold
Or dead to feeling—I will have pity on you.

Priest

King Oedipus, our master in Thebes, if you will look
At your altars, and at the ages of those who kneel there,
You will see children, too small to fly far from home;
You will see old men, slow with the years they carry,
And priests—I am a priest of Zeus; and you will see
The finest warriors you have; the rest of your people
Kneel, praying, in the open city, in the temples
Of Athene, and in the shrine where we keep a flame
Always alive and the ash whispers the future.
Look about you. The whole city drowns

And cannot lift its hand from the storm of death
In which it sinks: the green corn withers
In the fields, cattle die in the meadows,
Our wives weep in agony, and never give birth!
Apollo brings his fire like a drover and herds us
Into death, and nature is at war with herself.
Thebes is sick, every house deserted, and the blind
Prison of the dead grows rich with mourning
And our dying cries.
Eternal powers control our lives, and we do not
Think you are their equal; yet we pray to you, as
    your children,
Believing that you, more than any man, may direct
Events, and come to terms with the powers beyond us.
When the savage riddle of the Sphinx enslaved
Thebes, you came to set us free. We
Were powerless, we could not tell you how to
    answer her.
And now they say, and it is believed, that you
Were close to God when you raised our city from
    the dead.
Oedipus, we pray to your power, which can overcome
Sufferings we do not understand; guard us
From this evil. In heaven and earth there must
Be some answer to our prayer, and you may know it.
You have struggled once with the powers above us
    and been
Victorious; we trust that strength and believe
    your words.
Oedipus, you are the royal glory of Thebes—
Give us life; Oedipus—think. Because
You overpowered the evil in the Sphinx
We call you savior still. Must we remember
Your reign for the greatness in which you began,
    and the sorrow
In which you ended? The country is sick, and you
Must heal us. You were once our luck, our fortune,
    the augury
Of good we looked for in the world outside. Fulfil
That augury now. You are king of Thebes, but consider:
Which is it better to rule—a kingdom? Or a desert?

What is a castle or a ship if there are
No men to give it life? Emptiness! Nothing!

Oedipus

My children, I know your sorrows, I know why
You have come, and what you ask of me. I see
The pain of sickness in you all, and yet in all
That sickness, who is so sick as I? Each
Of you has one sorrow, his grief is his own—
But I must feel for my country, for myself,
And for you. That is why you did not find me
Deaf or indifferent to your prayers. No,
I have spent many tears, and in my thoughts
Traveled long journeys. And then I saw
That we could be saved in one way only;
I took that way and sent Creon, my brother-
In-law, to the Oracle of Apollo; there
The god will tell him how I can save the city—
The price may be an act of sacrifice, or perhaps
A vow, a prayer, will be enough. . . . But the days
Run on and the measure of time keeps pace with them
And I begin to fear. What is he doing?
I did not think he would stay so long—he should not
Stay so long! . . . But when he comes I will do
Whatever the god commands; if I disobeyed
It would be a sin.

Priest

           Heaven listened then;
This messenger says that Creon is returning.

Oedipus

My lord Apollo, let his news be the shining sun
That answers our prayers and guides us out of death!

Priest

I can see him now . . . the news must be good.
Look, there is a crown of bay thick with flowers
Covering his hair.

Oedipus

           At last we shall know the truth.
If I shout, he will hear me . . . Creon!
My brother, son of Menoeceus, Lord of Thebes,
What answer does Apollo send to us? Do you bring
An answer?

[*Enter* CREON.

Creon

        Our danger is gone. This load of sorrow
Will be lifted if we follow the way
Where Apollo points.

Oedipus

        What does this mean? I expected
Hope, or fear, but your answer gives me neither.

Creon

I am ready to tell you my message now, if you wish;
But they can hear us, and if we go inside . . .

Oedipus

Tell me now and let them hear! I must not think
Of myself; I grieve only when my people suffer.

Creon

Then this is what I was told at Delphi:
Our land is tainted. We carry the guilt in our midst.
A foul disease, which will not be healed unless
We drive it out and deny it life.

Oedipus

        But how
Shall we be clean? How did this happen to us?

Creon

The crime of murder is followed by a storm.
Banish the murder and you banish the storm, kill
Again and you kill the storm.

Oedipus

        But Apollo means
One man—who is this man?

Creon

        My lord,
There was once a king of Thebes; he was our master
Before you came to rule our broken city.

Oedipus

I have heard of him . . . I never saw your king.

Creon

Now that he is dead your mission from the god
Is clear: take vengeance on his murderers!

Oedipus

But where are they now? The crime is old,
And time is stubborn with its secrets. How

Can you ask me to find these men?

Creon

The god said
You must search in Thebes; what is hunted can
Be caught, only what we ignore escapes.

Oedipus

Where was the murder? Was Laius killed in the city?
Or did this happen in another country?

Creon

He was traveling
To Delphi, he said. But he never returned to the palace
He left that day.

Oedipus

Did no one see this?
A messenger? The guard who watched his journey?
You could
Have questioned them.

Creon

They were all killed, except
One. He ran home in terror, and could only
Repeat one thing.

Oedipus

What did he repeat?
Once we have learnt one thing, we may learn the rest.
This hope is the beginning of other hopes.

Creon

He said they met some robbers who killed the king.
He talked of an army, too strong for the servants
of Laius.

Oedipus

Robbers would not dare to kill a king—unless
They had bribes. They must have had bribes from
the city!

Creon

We suspected that, but with Laius dead
We were defenceless against our troubles.

Oedipus

Were
Your troubles so great that they prevented you
From knowing the truth? Your king had been
murdered . . . !

Creon

But the Sphinx
Had a riddle to which there was no answer, and
  we thought
Of our closest sorrows. We had no time for other
Mysteries.

Oedipus

But I will begin again, and make your
  mysteries
Plain. Apollo was right, and you were right,
To turn my thoughts to the king who died. Now
You will see the measure of my power; I come to
  defend you,
Avenging your country and the god Apollo.
[*Aside*] If I can drive out this corruption and make the city
Whole, I shall do more than save my people,
Who are my friends, but still my subjects—I shall save
Myself. For the knife that murdered Laius may yet
Drink from my heart, and the debt I pay to him
Lies to my own credit.
My children, quickly, leave this altar and take
Your branches. I will have the people of Thebes
  assembled
To hear that I shall do all the god commands.
And in the end we shall see my fortune smiling
From heaven, or my fall.
[*Exit* OEDIPUS.

Priest

Let us go, my sons; our king has given the order
We came to hear. May Apollo, who sent this answer
From his oracle, come to lay our sickness
To rest, and give us life.
[*Exeunt* PRIEST, CREON, *and some of the elders.*
[*Enter* CHORUS.

Chorus

From golden Delphi Apollo replies to Thebes
And the words of heaven send a warning.
As a lyre is strung and tightened, so we
Are tightened by fear.
As a lyre trembles, so we tremble at the touch of fear.
Apollo, god of healing, god of newness,

We fear you, and the commands you send to humble us.
Do you ask a new submission? Or is your command
The same as we hear in every wind, and every season,
    and every year?
Only the child of golden hope, whose voice
Will never die, only the spirit of truth can tell us.
First in my prayers is the goddess Athene, the
    daughter of Zeus;
Second, her sister Artemis, who is queen in Thebes,
For she sits at our country's heart, pure and honored,
In a temple like the sun. And third in our prayer
Is Phoebus Apollo, whose arm reaches over all the world.
Come three times to drive our wrongs before you!
If ever in the past, when evil and blindness
Rose like a wave, when grief was burning in our city,
If ever you banished that grief,
Come now to help us.
There is no numbering our sorrows;
The whole country is sick, and mortal will and
    human mind
Are no weapons to defend us.
The great earth whom we call our mother
Is barren and dead; women weep in the pain of
    childbirth
But they fall sick and die.
Look, can you see the dying go following each other,
Gliding like gentle birds, quicker
Then the restless flash of fire that will never sleep,
The dying on their flight to the shore
Where evening sits like a goddess?
The city of the dying goes countless away
And the children of life fall to the earth,
The toys of death,
With no pity and no remembering tears.

In the rest of our city wives and mothers
Stand gray at the altars,
Which tell us of a certainty resisting the seas of doubt;
They weep, pray, plead for release
From the harsh revenge which heaven brings.
A cry for healing rises and burns above the still crowd

That mourns in the city.
Send us strength that will look kindly on us,
Golden daughter of Zeus.
Ares, the god of war, confronts us, bitter in his cruelty,
And his shout burns like fire;
But his war is fought with no armor, and Ares
Carries no shield, for he brings his conflict
Into the moment of our birth and death.
Oh, turn him flying down the winds, turn him
Back and dash him from our country
Into the wide chambers where Amphitrite sleeps,
Or to the lonely cliffs of Thrace where the seas
Allow no guests. For Ares comes to finish
The deadly work left undone by the night.
Zeus, you are the lord of lightning, lord of fire,
Destroy him with your thunder, crush our enemy!

Lord Apollo, god in the sun, we pray for your light;
Strike with your golden spears and your hands of fire,
Strike to protect us.
We pray for Artemis to bring her chaste fires,
Which we see her carry like a shining torch across
The mountains where the wolf runs.
I call you, the god with the golden crown,
Born in our country, Bacchus,
With the fire of wine in your cheek,
And the voice of wine in your shout,
Come with your pine branch burning, and your Maenads
Following the light, the fire of heaven's madness
In their eyes, come to guard us against the
    treacherous power
Who goes to war with justice and the harmony
    of heaven!

[*Enter* OEDIPUS.

Oedipus

You have told me of your need. Are you content
To hear me speak, obey my words, and work
To humor the sickness? . . . Then you will thrust away
The weight with which you struggle, and fulfil
Your need. I am a stranger to this story,
And to the crime; I have no signs to guide me,

And so if I am to trap this murderer, my hunt
Must follow every hope. I am speaking, then,
To every citizen of Thebes, and I shall not
Exempt myself, although I am a citizen only
In name, and not in blood.
Whoever knows the murderer of Laius, son
Of Labdacus, must make his knowledge mine.
It is the king's command! And if he is afraid,
Or thinks he will escape, I say to him, "Speak!
You will go into exile, but you will go unharmed—
Banishment is all you have to fear."
Or if you know the assassin comes from another
Country, you must not be silent. I shall pay
The value of your knowledge, and your reward
Will be more than gratitude.
But if I find only silence, if you are afraid
To betray a friend or reveal yourself, and lock
The truth away, listen, this is my decree:
This murderer, no matter who he is, is banished
From the country where my power and my throne
Are supreme. No one must shelter him or speak to him;
When you pray to heaven, he must not pray with you;
When you sacrifice, drive him away, do not
Give him holy water, beat him from your doors!
He carries the taint of corruption with him—for so
The god Apollo has revealed to me. . . . You see
How I serve the god and revenge the king who died!
I curse that murderer; if he is alone, I curse him!
If he shares his guilt with others, I curse him! May
His evil heart beat out its years in sorrow,
Throughout his life may he breathe the air of death!
If I give him shelter, knowing who
He is, and let him feel the warmth of my fire,
I ask this punishment for myself.
This must be done! In every word I speak
I command obedience, and so does the god Apollo,
And so does your country, which a barren sickness
And an angry heaven drag to death. But even
If it is not a god that comes to punish you
It would be shame to leave your land impure.
Your king was killed—he was a royal and noble

Man; hunt his murderer down!
I live in Laius' palace, my queen was once
The queen of Laius, and if his line had prospered
His children would have shared my love.
But now time has struck his head to earth
And in revenge I will fight for him as I
Would fight for my own father. My search will never
End until I take in chains the murderer
Of Laius, son of Labdacus. I pray heaven
That those who will not help me may watch the soil
They have ploughed crumble and turn black, let
    them see
Their women barren, let them be destroyed by the fury
That scourges us, but may it rage more cruelly!
And for all the Thebans who will obey me gladly
I ask the strength of justice, and the power of heaven.
So we shall live in peace; so we shall be healed.

Chorus
Your curse menaces me, my lord, if I lie.
I swear I did not kill him, nor can I tell
Who did. Apollo sent the reply, and Apollo
Should find the murderer.

Oedipus
                   Yes, we believe
It is Apollo's task—but we cannot make
The gods our slaves; we must act for ourselves.

Chorus
                             Our next
Hope, then, must be . . .

Oedipus
                 And every hope
You have. When I search, nothing escapes.

Chorus
We know a lord who sees as clearly as the lord
Apollo—Teiresias; we could ask Teiresias, my king,
And be given the truth.

Oedipus
               Creon told me, and his advice
Did not lie idle for want of action. I have sent
Two servants. . . . It is strange they are not here.

Chorus
And there are the old rumors—but they tell
   us nothing . . .
Oedipus
What do these rumors say? I must know
Everything.
Chorus
        They say some travelers killed him.
Oedipus
I have heard that too. But the man who saw those
   travelers
Was never seen himself.
Chorus
         The murderer will leave our country;
There is a part of every man that is ruled
By fear, and when he hears your curse . . .
Oedipus
                    A sentence
Holds no terror for the man who is not afraid
To kill.
Chorus
But now he will be convicted. Look,
They are leading your priest to you; Teiresias comes.
When he speaks, it is the voice of heaven
That we hear.
[*Enter* TEIRESIAS, *guided by a boy.*
Oedipus
             Teiresias, all things lie
In your power, for you have harnessed all
Knowledge and all mysteries; you know what heaven
Hides, and what runs in the earth below, and you
Must know, though you cannot see, the sickness
   with which
Our country struggles. Defend us, my lord, and
   save us—
We shall find no other defence or safety.
For Apollo—and yet you must have heard the message—
Apollo, whom we asked in our doubt, promised release—
But on one condition: that we find the murderers
Of Laius, and banish them, or repay the murder.
Teiresias, the singing birds will tell you of the future,

You have many ways of knowing the truth. Do
   not grudge
Your knowledge, but save yourself and your city,
   save me,
For murder defiles us all. Think of us
As your prisoners, whose lives belong to you!
To have the power and use that power for good
Is work to bring you honor.

Teiresias

                  When truth cannot help
The man who knows, then it brings terror. I knew
That truth, but I stifled it. I should not have come.

Oedipus

What is it? You come as sadly as despair.

Teiresias

Send me away, I tell you! Then it will be easy
For you to play the king, and I the priest.

Oedipus

This is no reply. You cannot love Thebes—your own
Country, Teiresias—if you hide what the gods tell you.

Teiresias

I see your words guiding you on the wrong
Path; I pray for my own escape.

Oedipus

                Teiresias!
You do not turn away if you know the truth; we all
Come like slaves to a king with our prayers to you.

Teiresias

But you come without the truth, and I can never
Reveal my own sorrows, lest they become
Yours.

Oedipus

You cannot? Then you know and will not tell us!
Instead, you plan treason and the city's death.

Teiresias

I mean to protect us both from pain. You search
And probe, and it is all wasted. I will not tell you!

Oedipus

You demon! You soul of evil! You would goad
A thing of stone to fury. Will you never speak?
Can you feel, can you suffer? Answer me, and end this!

Teiresias
You see wrong in my mood, you call me evil—blind
To the mood that settles in you and rages there.

Oedipus
Rages! Yes, that is what your words
Have done, when they shout your contempt for Thebes.

Teiresias
The truth will come; my silence cannot hide it.

Oedipus
And what must come is what you must tell me.

Teiresias
I can tell you no more, and on this answer let
Your fury caper like a beast.

Oedipus

It is
A fury that will never leave me. Listen, I know
What you are. I see now that you conspired to plan
This murder, and you committed it—all but the stroke
That killed him. If you had eyes, I would have said
The crime was yours alone.

Teiresias

Oedipus, I warn you!
Obey your own decree and the oath you swore.
Never from this day speak to me, or to these nobles;
You are our corruption, the unholiness in our land.

Oedipus
How you must despise me to flaunt your scorn like this,
Thinking you will escape. How?

Teiresias

I have escaped.
I carry the truth; it is my child, and guards me.

Oedipus
Truth! Who taught you? Heaven never taught you!

Teiresias
You taught me; you forced me to the point of speech.

Oedipus
Repeat your words, I do not remember this speech.

Teiresias
You did not understand? Or do you try to trap me?

Oedipus
I know nothing! Repeat your truth!

Teiresias

    I said, you are the murderer you are searching for.

Oedipus

    Again you attack me, but I will not forgive you again!

Teiresias

    Shall I say more to make your anger sprawl?

Oedipus

    All you have breath for—it will all be useless.

Teiresias

    Then . . . you live with your dearest one in burning
    Shame, and do not know it; nor can you see
    The evil that surrounds you.

Oedipus

                    Do you think
    You will always smile in freedom if you talk like this?

Teiresias

    If truth can give strength, I will.

Oedipus

                    It can—
    But not to you; you have no truth. Your senses
    Have died in you—ears: deaf! eyes: blind!

Teiresias

    Yes, be bitter, mock at me, poor Oedipus.
    Soon they will all mock as bitterly at you.

Oedipus

    You live in perpetual night; you cannot harm
    Me, nor anyone who moves in the light.

Teiresias

                  Your downfall
    Will come, but I will not be the cause. Apollo
    Is a great power; he watches over the end.

Oedipus

    Did you or Creon plan this?

Teiresias

               Creon is not
    Your enemy; you carry your enemy with you—
        in your soul.

Oedipus

    We have wealth and power, the mind reaches
        higher, grows,
    Breaks its own fetters, our lives are great and envied,

And the world rewards us—with spitefulness and hate!
Consider my power—I did not come begging, the city
Laid its submisson in my hands as a gift.
Yet, for this power, Creon, my trusted, my first
Friend, goes like a thief behind my back,
Tries to exile me, and sends this wizard,
This patcher of threadbare stories, this cunning peddler
Of the future, with no eyes except
For money, and certainly no eyes for mysteries.
Tell me, tell me, when did you ever foretell the truth?
When the Sphinx howled her mockeries and riddles
Why could you find no answer to free the city?
Her question was too hard for the simple man,
The humble man; only heaven's wisdom could find
A reply. But you found none! Neither your birds
Above you, nor the secret voice of your inspiration
Sent you knowledge—then we saw what you were!
But I came, ignorant Oedipus, and silenced her,
And my only weapon was in my mind and my will;
I had no omens to teach me. And this is the man
You would usurp! You think, when Creon is king
You will sit close to the throne; but I think
Your plans to drive the accursed away will return
To defeat you, and to defeat their architect.
You are old, Teiresias, or else your prophetic wisdom
Would have been your death.

Chorus

>   Your majesty, what he has said
And your reply—they were both born in anger.
We do not need this wildness; we ask the best
Fulfilment of Apollo's commands. This must be
    the search.

Teiresias

[*To* OEDIPUS] You flourish your power; but you must give
    me the right
To make my reply, and that will have equal power.
I have not lived to be your servant, but Apollo's;
Nor am I found in the list of those whom Creon
Protects. You call me blind, you jeer at me—
I say your sight is not clear enough to see

Who shares your palace, nor the rooms in which
   you walk,
Nor the sorrow about you. Do you know who gave
   you birth?
You are the enemy of the dead, and of the living,
And do not know it. The curse is a two-edged sword,
From your mother, from your father; the curse will
   hunt you,
Like a destruction, from your country. Now
You have sight, but then you will go in blindness;
When you know the truth of your wedding night
All the world will bear your crying to rest,
Every hill a Cithaeron to echo you.
You thought that night was peace, like a gentle harbor—
But there was no harbor for that voyage, only grief.
Evil crowds upon you; you do not see
How it will level you with your children and reveal
Yourself as you truly are. Howl your abuse
At Creon and at me. . . . All men must suffer,
Oedipus, but none will find suffering more terrible
Than you.

Oedipus

                    Must I bear this? Must I be silent?
Die! Go to your death! Leave my palace now!
Get away from me!

Teiresias

Yet you called me here, or I would not have come.

Oedipus

If I had known you would talk in the raving language
Of a madman, I would never have sent for you.

Teiresias

I am no more than you see. You see a madman,
The parents who gave you life saw a prophet.

Oedipus

My parents? Wait! Who were my parents?

Teiresias

Today will be your parent, and your murderer.

Oedipus

Always riddles, always lies and riddles!

Teiresias

You were best at solving riddles, were you not?

Oedipus

When you think of my greatness, it inspires your
mockery.

Teiresias

That greatness has conspired to be your traitor.

Oedipus

I saved this country, I care for nothing else.

Teiresias

Then I shall go. . . . [*To his guide*] Boy, lead me away.

Oedipus

Yes, lead him. . . . You come and trouble me—
you are nothing
But hindrance to my plans. Go, and I shall be safe.

Teiresias

I came to speak, and I shall not leave until I speak.
I need not cower at your frown, you cannot
Harm me. This man for whom you search,
Whom you threaten, and to the people call
"the murderer
Of Laius," this man is here, a stranger, a foreigner;
But he will see his Theban blood, though he will not
Have any joy at the discovery.
He will be blind—though now he sees; a beggar—
Though now he is rich, and he will go feeling
Strange ground before him with a stick.
He is a father to children—then he will
Be called their brother; he is his mother's son—
Then he will be called her husband, then
He will be called his father's murderer.
Consider this when you walk between your palace walls;
If you find I have been false to you, then say
That all my prophetic wisdom is a lie.

[*Exeunt all but the* CHORUS.

Chorus

In the rock at Delphi there is a cave
Which is the mouth of heaven; now
The cave warns us of one man, whose hands are red
With murder, and whose actions
Break the unspoken laws that shackle us.
Time tells him now to escape,
Faster than the jostling horses of the storm,

For Apollo, the son of Zeus, leaps down on him,
Armed with lightning, dressed in fire,
And the terrible avengers follow where he goes,
The Furies who never mistake and are never cheated.
From the snow of Parnassus over Delphi the message
Gleamed and came shining to Thebes.
We must all hunt the murderer
Who hides from justice. Like a lonely bull
He crosses and crosses our country, through the
    harsh forests,
The hollows of the mountains, and the rocks.
Sadly trying to escape
The words that came from Delphi, the heart of
  the world.
But their wings are always beating in his head.

The wisdom of the priest sets fear, fear, beating in
    our blood;
Truth or lies, nothing comforts, nothing denies.
The world is built out of our beliefs,
And when we lose those beliefs in doubt,
Our world is destroyed, and the present and the past
Vanish into night.
We must have proof, a certainty that we can touch
And feel, before we turn against Oedipus.
The land is peopled with rumors and whispers—
They cannot make us avenge King Laius,
Whose death is guarded by such mystery.

All that men may do is watched and remembered
By Zeus, and by Apollo. But they are gods;
Can any man, even the prophet, the priest,
Can even he know more than us?
And if he can, who will be judge of him, and say he lied
Or spoke the truth.
Yet wisdom may come to us, not the wisdom that sees
How the world is ruled, but the wisdom that guides
The modest life. In this alone we may excel.
But the proof must be clear and certain,
Before I can accuse Oedipus.
Remember that the Sphinx came flying

To meet him, evil beyond our comprehension,
And we saw his wisdom then, we knew and felt
The goodness of his heart towards our country.
Thoughts cannot be guilty traitors to such a man.

[*Enter* CREON.

Creon

Lords of Thebes, this message has called me here
In terror. . . . These crimes of which our king
    accuses me—
No one would dare to think of them! If he
Believes I could wrong him, or even speak of wrong,
At such a time, when we are in such sorrow,
Let me die! I have no wish to live out my years
If I must live them suspected and despised.
I will not bear this slander, which is no trifle
To forget, but the greatest injury—the name
Of traitor. The people will call me that, even
You will call me that!

Chorus

               His fury mastered him;
Perhaps he did not mean the charge.

Creon

                      He said
To you all—you all heard—that the priest
Had been told to lie, and that I had planned the answer?

Chorus

He said that, but I know he did not mean it.

Creon

                     And when he
Accused me, he seemed master of his thoughts, and
    there was
Reason in his voice?

Chorus

             I cannot remember,
I do not observe my king so closely. . . . But here
He comes from the palace himself to meet you.

[*Enter* OEDIPUS.

Oedipus

                     So,
My citizen, you have come to your king? Your eyes
    have great

Courage—they can look on my palace out of a murderer's
Face, a robber's face! Yes, I know you;
You blaze, you thief of power . . . In heaven's name
Tell me: when you planned to kill me, did you think
    I had
Become a coward or a fool? Did you think I would not
Notice your treason stalking me? Or were you sure
That if I knew, I would not dare defence?
See your insane attempt! You try to capture
Power, which must be hunted with armies and gold;
But no one will follow you, no one will make
You rich!

Creon

            Wait! You have accused, but you must
                 not judge
Until you have heard my defence; I can reply.

Oedipus

You talk with the fangs of cleverness; but how
Can I understand? I understand only
That you are my enemy, and dangerous.

Creon

There is one thing I must say; hear it first.

Oedipus

One thing you must not say: "I am innocent."

Creon

You are stubborn, Oedipus, your will is too hard;
It is nothing to treasure, and you are wrong to think it is.

Oedipus

Treason, crimes against a brother, will not
Escape justice: you are wrong to think they will.

Creon

I do not quarrel with your talk of justice.
But tell me how I have harmed you: what is my crime?

Oedipus

Did you persuade me—perhaps you did not—to send for
The priest whom we used to worship for his wisdom?

Creon

And I still have faith in that advice.

Oedipus

                      How long

Is it since Laius . . .

Creon
                              What has Laius to do
With this? I do not see . . .

Oedipus
                              Since he was hidden
From the living sun, since he was attacked and killed?

Creon
The years are old and the time is long since then.

Oedipus
Was Teiresias already a priest and prophet then?

Creon
As wise as now, and no less honored and obeyed.

Oedipus
But at the time he did not mention me?

Creon
I did not hear him. . . .

Oedipus
                              But surely you tried to find
The murderer?

Creon
                    We searched, of course, we could discover
Nothing.

Oedipus
          If I was guilty, why did Teiresias
Not accuse me then? He must have known, for he is wise.

Creon
I do not know. If I cannot know the truth
I would rather be silent.

Oedipus
                              But there is one truth
You will confess to; none knows it better . . . ?

Creon
What is that? I shall deny nothing. . . .

Oedipus
That only by some insidious plan of yours
Could Teiresias ever say I murdered Laius!

Creon
If he says that, I cannot unsay it for him;
But give me an answer in return for mine.

Oedipus
Question till you have no questions left;

You cannot prove me a murderer.
Creon

                            Now,
You have married my sister?
Oedipus

                                  I do not deny it; the truth
Was in your question.
Creon

                         You and she rule
This country, you are equal?
Oedipus

                             If she has a wish
I grant it all to her.
Creon

                    And am I not
Considered equal to you both?
Oedipus

                          Yes, there your friendship
Shows the face of evil it concealed.
Creon
No, reason to yourself as I have reasoned.
First, imagine two ways of ruling, each
Bringing equal power. With one of these fear
Never leaves you, but with the other you sleep
Calm in the night. Who do you think
Would not choose the second? I feel no ambition
To be the king, when I have the power of a king.
For I have my place in the world, I know it, and will not
Overreach myself. Now, you give me all
I wish, and no fear comes with the gift;
But if I were king myself, much more would be forced
Upon me. Why should I love the throne better
Than a throne's power and a throne's majesty
Without the terrors of a throne? Now,
I may smile to all, and all will bow to me;
Those who need you petition me,
For I am their hopes of success. Is this such a worthless
Life that I should exchange it for yours? Treason
Is for those who cannot value what they have.
I have never had longing thoughts about your power,
Nor would I help a man who had. Send

To Delphi, make a test of me, ask the god
Whether my message was true, and if you find
I have plotted with your priest, then you may kill me—
I will be your authority, I will assent
When you decree my death. But do not accuse me
Yet, when you know nothing. You wrong your friends
To think them enemies, as much as you do wrong
To take enemies for friends. Think, be sure!
You banish life from your body—and life you love
Most dearly—by banishing a good friend.
Time will set this knowledge safely in your heart;
Time alone shows the goodness in a man—
One day is enough to tell you all his evil.

Chorus
My king, a cautious man would listen; beware
Of being convinced too quickly. Suddenness is not safety.

Oedipus
When the attack is quick and sudden, and the plot
Runs in the darkness, my thoughts must be sudden
In reply. If I wait, sitting in silence,
He will have done his work, and I lost
My chance to begin.

Creon

                Your decision then! Will you
Banish me?

Oedipus

           No, not banishment; I
Will have your life! You must teach men the rewards
That I keep for the envious and the cruel.

Creon
Will you not listen to persuasion and the truth?

Oedipus
You will never persuade me that you speak the truth.

Creon
No, I can see you are blind to truth.

Oedipus

                    I see
Enough to guard my life.

Creon

                My life is as precious
To me.

Oedipus
But you are a traitor!

Creon
You know nothing!

Oedipus
Yet the king must rule.

Creon
Not when the king is evil.

Oedipus
My city! My city!

Creon
It is my city too, do not forget that!

Chorus
Stop, my lords! Look, here is Jocasta coming to you
From the palace, at the moment when she may help you
To bring this quarrel to rest.

[*Enter* JOCASTA.

Jocasta
My lords, it is pitiful to hear your senseless voices
Shouting and wrangling. Have you no shame?
Our country
Is sick, and you go bustling about your private
Quarrels. My king, you must go inside, and you,
Creon, go to the palace. At this time
We have no troubles except the plague; all
Others are pretence.

Creon
My sister, your sovereign, Oedipus,
Condemns me cruelly in his efforts to be just.
He will banish me, or murder me; in both he does wrong.

Oedipus
No, I have found a traitor, my queen, who plots
Against my life.

Creon
Never let me breathe
In freedom again, let me die under your curse,
If I am guilty of those crimes!

Jocasta
Oh, Oedipus,
Believe him. Believe him for the sake of those words
Which heaven witnessed; you have a duty to that oath,

And to me, and to your people.

Chorus

Obey her, my lord, I beg you; do not be harsh,
Be wise.

Oedipus

Must I be ruled by you?

Chorus

Creon was always wise and faithful in the past; his oath
was great
And you must respect it.

Oedipus

You know what you are asking?

Chorus

I know.

Oedipus

Tell me, what do you advise?

Chorus

He is your friend—that is a truth
As simple as the light of day;
But only confused and uncertain rumors call him traitor;
No cause to rob him of his honor.

Oedipus

But listen, in asking this, you ask
For my banishment, or for my death.

Chorus

No! By the sun who is prince of the sky!
If that was ever my intention,
I pray for death, without friends on earth
Without love in heaven,
Death in pain and misery.
Now, now, when the decaying earth eats our lives
Away, will you add your quarrels to all
That we already suffer?

Oedipus

Let him go then; I shall die, I do not care;
I shall be driven into banishment and disgrace.
I do this for love and pity of you. For him, I feel none;
Wherever he goes, he cannot escape my hatred.

Creon

For you submission is a torment—you do not hide it.
And when you force your way against the world

You crush us all beneath you. Such natures
Find their own company most terrible to bear.
It is their punishment.

Oedipus

Leave my sight, then! Leave me to myself!

Creon

I shall leave you. In all the time you knew me,
You never understood me. . . . They see my innocence.

[*Exit* CREON.

Chorus

My queen, take our king to the palace now.

Jocasta

I must know what has happened.

Chorus

Doubt and suspicion. Oedipus spoke without thinking;
He was unjust, and Creon cannot bear injustice.

Jocasta

Both were to blame?

Chorus

                                    Yes.

Jocasta

                                    What was said?

Chorus

The country is weary with sickness already;
I am content, content to go no further
And let the evil rest.

Oedipus

You see what you have done, you good,
Good adviser? My temper was a spear
And you have turned the edge and blunted it.

Chorus

Your majesty, I have repeated many times—
But I tell you again;
I would have been robbed of all my senses,
Emptied of all my reason,
If I caused your death.
You came like the wind we pray for in danger,
When the storm was conquering us with sorrows,
And carried our country into safety. Again
You may bring a spirit to guide us.

Jocasta

But I still do not know why you were quarreling, my king,
And I must know, for they talked of your death.

Oedipus

Jocasta,

You may command me when even my people may not,
And I let Creon go. But he had conspired
Against me. . . .

Jocasta

Treason! Is this true? Can you prove it?

Oedipus

He says I am Laius' murderer.

Jocasta

How

Can he know? Has he always known, or has someone
told him?

Oedipus

He sent that priest Teiresias, the wicked Teiresias.
Creon's lips do not commit themselves to words!

Jocasta

Then set all this talk aside and listen. I
Will teach you that no priest, no holy magic
Can know your future or your destiny. And my proof
Is as short as the stroke of a knife. Once, an oracle
Came to Laius—I will not say it was from
Apollo—but from Apollo's priests. It told him
He was destined to be murdered by the son that I
Would bear to him. But Laius, so they say,
Was murdered by robbers from another country
at a place
Where three roads meet. A son was born
To us, but lived no more than three days. Yes,
Laius pinned his ankles together and sent him
Away to die on a distant, lonely mountain.
Once he was there, no power could make
him a murderer,
Nor make Laius die at the hands of his son—
And he feared that above anything in the world.
You see how you may rely upon priests and their talk
Of the future. Never notice them! When god wishes
The truth discovered, he will easily work his will.

Oedipus

As I listened, my queen, my thoughts went reaching
    out
And touched on memories that make me shudder. . . .

Jocasta

What memories? You stare as if you were trapped.

Oedipus

You said—I heard you say—that Laius' blood
Was spilt at a place where three roads meet.

Jocasta

We were all told that, and no one has denied it.

Oedipus

And where is the place where this happened?

Jocasta

                                    The country
Is called Phocis; the road splits, to Delphi
And to Daulia.

Oedipus

                When did all this happen?

Jocasta

The city was given the news a little before
You became king of Thebes.

Oedipus

                        God,
What do you hold prepared for me?

Jocasta

                            Oedipus!
What made you frown when I talked of your becoming
    king?

Oedipus

Do not ask me yet. . . . Laius—what was he like?
His appearance, his age, describe them to me.

Jocasta

He was tall, his hair beginning to be flecked with a down
Of white; he was built like you. . . .

Oedipus

                            Stop! You torture me!
I have hurled myself blindly against unthinking
Fury and destruction!

Jocasta

                How? I cannot bear

To watch you, my lord.

Oedipus

        So little hope is frightening.
Listen, Teiresias the priest was not blind!
But one more answer, one more, will be better proof.

Jocasta

I dare not answer; but if my answers help you,
Ask.

Oedipus

When he left Thebes, was he alone,
Or did he have a company of men at arms
So that all could recognize he was a king?

Jocasta

No, five were all the travelers, and one
Was a herald. A single chariot carried Laius. . . .

Oedipus

Yes! Now I see the truth. . . . Who told you this?

Jocasta

A servant, the only man who returned alive.

Oedipus

Is he still in the palace with us?

Jocasta

          No, after
He escaped, and found that you were king, and Laius
Dead, he implored me by my duty to a suppliant
To send him away. To the country, he said, herding
Sheep on the hillsides, where he could never see
The city he had left. . . . And I let him go; he was
A good servant, deserving more than this
Small favor.

Oedipus

       He must be found at once;
Can this be done?

Jocasta

Yes, but why do you want him?

Oedipus

My queen, as I look into myself I begin to fear;
I had no right to say those things, and so
I must see this man.

Jocasta

        He will come. But I

Expect to be told your sorrows, my king, when they
weigh
So heavily.

Oedipus

And I will not refuse you, Jocasta.
I have come to face such thoughts, and who should hear
Of them before you? I walk among
Great menaces.
My father is king of Corinth—Polybus; my mother—
Merope from Doris. In Corinth I was called
Their prince, their greatest noble, until
This happened to me—it was strange, yet not
So strange as to deserve my thoughts so much.
A man, stuffed with wine at a feast, called out
To me as he drank. He said I was a son only
In the imagination of my father. Anger
And pain would not let me rest that day; the next
I went to my parents and questioned them. They
answered
The drunkard harshly for his insulting story,
And for their sakes I was glad he lied. Yet I always
Felt the wound, and the story spread in whispers.
At last I went to Delphi—my parents did not know—
But Apollo thought me unworthy of an answer
To that question. Instead he foretold many trials,
Many dangers, many sorrows. I was to be
My mother's husband, I was to murder my own
Father, my children would carry the guilt and none
Would dare look on them. When I heard this
I ran from my home and afterwards knew the land
Only by the stars that stood above it.
Never must I see the shame of that evil prophecy
Acted out by me in Corinth. I traveled
Until I came to this place where you say your king
Was killed. . . . My wife, this is the truth. . . . I will tell
you. . . .
My journey brought me to the meeting of three roads;
And there a herald, and an old man who rode
A chariot drawn by mares, came towards me. . . .
Jocasta, the rider was like the man you described!
He and the herald, who went in front, tried

To force me out of their path. In a rage I struck
The one who touched me, the servant at the wheel.
The old man watched me, and waited till I was passing;
Then from the chariot he aimed at the crown of my head
With the twin prongs of his goad. It was a costly
Action! Slashing with my stick I cut at him
And my blow tumbled him backwards out
    of the chariot—
Then I killed them all! If this man I met may be said
To resemble Laius, to be, perhaps, Laius,
I stand condemned to more sorrow than any man,
More cursed by an evil power than any man.
No one in Thebes, no stranger, may shelter me
Or speak to me; they must hunt me from their doors.
And I, it was I, who cursed myself, cursed myself!
And the dead king's pillow is fouled by the touch
Of my murdering hands. Is the evil in my soul?
Is my whole nature tainted? Must I go into exile,
Never see my people again, nor turn home
And set foot in Corinth?—for if I do, I must wed
My mother, and kill my father—Polybus, who gave me
Life and youth. Can you see this happen, and then
Deny that a cruel power has come to torture me?
No! You heavens, you pure light and holiness!
Let me die before that day, hide me before
I feel that black corruption in my soul!

Chorus

My king, this is a frightening story. But hope,
Until you hear from the man who saw what happened.

Oedipus

Yes, that is all the hope I have. Oedipus
Waits for one man, and he is a shepherd.

Jocasta

What makes you so eager for him to come?

Oedipus

I reason like this. We may find that his story
Matches yours. Then I shall be as free
As if this had never happened.

Jocasta

                      Was there anything in what
I said that could have such power?

Oedipus

You said
He told you robbers murdered Laius. If he still
Says "robbers" and not "a robber," I am innocent.
One man cannot be taken for many.
But if he says a murderer, alone,
The guilt comes to rest on me.

Jocasta

But we all
Heard him say "robbers"; that is certain. He cannot
Unsay it. I am not alone, for the whole city heard.
But even if he swerves a little from his old account,
That will not prove you Laius' murderer,
Not in truth, not in justice. For Apollo said
He was to be killed by a son that was born to me . . .
And yet my son, poor child, could not have killed him,
For he died first . . . but that shows the deceit
Of prophecies. They beckon at you, but I
Would fix my eyes ahead, and never look at them!

Oedipus

You are right. Nevertheless send someone
To bring me that servant; do not forget.

Jocasta

Yes,
I will send now. Let us go to the palace;
I would do nothing that could harm or anger you.

[*Exeunt all but the* CHORUS

Chorus

All actions must beware of the powers beyond us,
    and each word
Must speak our fear of heaven. I pray
That I may live every hour in obedience.
The laws that hold us in subjection
Have always stood beyond our reach, conceived
In the high air of heaven. Olympus
Was their sire, and no woman on earth
Gave them life. They are laws
That will never be lured to sleep in the arms of oblivion,
And in their strength heaven is great and cannot
    grow old.
Yet man desires to be more than man, to rule

His world for himself.
This desire, blown to immensity
On the rich empty food of its ambition,
Out of place, out of time,
Clambers to the crown of the rock, and stands there,
Tottering; then comes the steepling plunge down
    to earth,
To the earth where we are caged and mastered.
But this desire may work for good
When it fights to save a country, and I pray
That heaven will not weaken it then.
For then it comes like a god to be our warrior
And we shall never turn it back.

Justice holds the balance of all things,
And we must fear her.
Do not despise the frontiers in which we must live,
Do not cross them, do not talk of them,
But bow before the places where the gods are throned.
Time will come with cruel vengeance on the man
Who disobeys; that is the punishment
For those who are proud and are more than men—
They are humbled
If a man grows rich in defiance of this law,
If his actions trespass on a world that he should fear,
If he reaches after mysteries that no man should know,
No prayer can plead for him when the sword of heaven
    is raised.
If he were to glory in success
All worship would fall dumb.

Delphi is the heart of the world and holds its secrets;
The temple of Zeus, and Olympia, command our prayers;
But we shall never believe again
Until the truth of this murder is known.
Let us be sure of our beliefs, give us proof.
Zeus, you may do your will; do not forget that
    you are immortal,
Your empire cannot die; hear our prayers.
For the oracle given to Laius in the years of
    the long past

Is dying and forgotten, wiped from the memory,
Apollo's glory turns to shadows,
And all divinity to ruin.

[*Enter* JOCASTA

Jocasta

My lords, I have been summoned by my thoughts
To the temples of the gods, and I have brought
These garlands and this incense for an offering.
Oedipus is like a lonely bird among
The terrors that flock about his mind. He forgets
His wisdom, and no longer thinks the past
    will guide him
When he tries to foresee the future. Instead, he is
The slave of any word that talks of fear.
I try to reach him, to make him see that there is hope,
But it is useless; I have failed. And so I turn
To you, Apollo, nearest to us in Thebes,
A suppliant with prayers and gifts. Resolve this doubt
By sending the truth. He is the guide and master
Of our ship. What shall we do when even he
Is struck into bewilderment?

[*Enter* MESSENGER.

Messenger

I do not know this country. Will you show me the palace
Of King Oedipus? I must find King Oedipus. . . .
Do you know where he is?

Chorus

                 This is his palace, sir.
He is inside, and you see his queen before you.

Messenger

Heaven give her and all she loves riches
And happiness if she is the queen of such a king.

Jocasta

I return your greeting. You have spoken well and deserve
Well wishing. But what do you want with Oedipus?
Or do you bring a message for us?

Messenger

                 A message
Of good, for your palace and your husband, my queen.

Jocasta

What is it? Who sent you here?

Messenger

I come from Corinth.
My story may be quickly told. You will be glad, of
course,
For the news is glad, and yet . . . yet you may grieve.

Jocasta
Well, what is this story with a double meaning?

Messenger
The people of Corinth—it was already announced
There—will make Oedipus their king.

Jocasta

But why?
Your king is Polybus. He is wise, revered . . .

Messenger
But no longer our king. Death hugs him to the earth.

Jocasta
Is this true? Polybus is dead?

Messenger
By my hopes of living out my years, it is true.

Jocasta
Servant, go, tell this to your master. Run!
[*Exit* SERVANT.
Where are the prophecies of heaven now? Always
Oedipus dreaded to kill this man, and hid
From him. But look, Polybus has been murdered
By the careless touch of time, and not by Oedipus.
[*Enter* OEDIPUS.

Oedipus
Dear Jocasta, dear wife, why have you called me
Here from the palace?

Jocasta

This man brings a message;
Listen, and then ask yourself what comes
Of the oracles from heaven that used to frighten us.

Oedipus
Who is this man? What has he to say to me?

Jocasta
He comes from Corinth, and his message is the death
Of Polybus. You will never see Polybus again!

Oedipus
You said that, stranger? Let me hear you say that plainly.

Messenger

Since you force me to give that part of my message first,
I repeat, he walks among the dead.

Oedipus

A plot?
Or did sickness conspire to kill him?

Messenger

A small
Touch on the balance sends old lives to sleep.

Oedipus

So, my poor father, sickness murdered you.

Messenger

And many years had measured out his life.

Oedipus

Oh look, look, who would listen to Apollo
Talking in his shrine at Delphi, or notice birds
That clamor to the air? They were the signs
That told me—and I believed—that I would kill
My father. But now he has the grave to protect him,
While I stand here, and I never touched a sword . . .
Unless he died of longing to see me—
Then perhaps he died because of me. No!
Polybus lies in darkness, and all those prophecies
Lie with him, chained and powerless.

Jocasta

I told you long ago how it would happen. . . .

Oedipus

Yes, but I was led astray by fears.

Jocasta

Then think no more of them; forget them all.

Oedipus

Not all. The marriage with my mother—I think of it.

Jocasta

But is there anything a man need fear, if he knows
That chance is supreme throughout the world, and
        he cannot
See what is to come? Give way to the power
Of events and live as they allow! It is best.
Do not fear this marriage with your mother. Many
Men have dreams, and in those dreams they wed
Their mothers. Life is easiest, if you do not try

To oppose these things which seem to threaten us.

Oedipus
You are right, and I would agree with all
You say, if my mother were not alive. And though
You are right, I must fear. She is alive.

Jocasta
Think of your father, and his grave.
There is a light to guide you.

Oedipus
It does guide me!
I know he . . . But she is alive and I am afraid.

Messenger
You are afraid of a woman, my lord?

Oedipus
Yes,
Merope—Polybus was her husband.

Messenger
How can you be afraid of her?

Oedipus
A prophecy warned me
To beware of sorrow. . . .

Messenger
Can you speak of it, or are you
Forbidden to talk of these things to others?

Oedipus
No,
I am not forbidden. The Oracle at Delphi
Has told me my destiny—to be my mother's husband
And my father's murderer. And so I left
Corinth, many years ago and many
Miles behind me. The world has rewarded me richly,
And yet all those riches are less than the sight
Of a parent's face.

Messenger
And you went into exile because
You feared this marriage?

Oedipus
And to save myself from becoming
My father's murderer.

Messenger
Then, my king,

I ought to have freed you from that fear since I
Wished to be thought your friend.
Oedipus

                             Your reward
Will be measured by my gratitude.
Messenger

                          I had hoped for reward
When you returned as king of your palace in Corinth.
Oedipus
I must never go where my parents are.
Messenger

                               My son,
You do not know what you say; I see you do not.
Oedipus
How, sir? Tell me quickly.
Messenger

                           . . . If you live in exile
Because of Polybus and Merope.
Oedipus

                             Yes, and I live
In fear that Apollo will prove he spoke the truth.
Messenger
And it is from your parents that the guilt is to come?
Oedipus
Yes, stranger, the fear never leaves my side.
Messenger
You have no cause to be afraid—do you know that?
Oedipus
No cause? But they were my parents—that is the cause!
Messenger
No cause, because they were not your parents, Oedipus.
Oedipus
What do you mean? Polybus was not my father?
Messenger
As much as I, and yet no more than I am.
Oedipus
How could my father be no more than nothing?
Messenger
But Polybus did not give you life, nor did I.
Oedipus
Then why did he call me son?

Messenger

Listen, you were
A gift that he took from my hands.

Oedipus

A child
Given him by a stranger? But he loved me
Dearly.

Messenger

He had no children, and so consented.

Oedipus

So you gave me to ... Had you bought me for your
slave
Where did you find me?

Messenger

You were lying beneath the trees
In a glade upon Cithaeron.

Oedipus

What were you doing on Cithaeron?

Messenger

My flocks were grazing in the mountains;
I was guarding them.

Oedipus

Guarding your flocks—you were
A shepherd, a servant!

Messenger

It was in that service that I saved
Your life, my child.

Oedipus

Why? Was I hurt or sick
When you took me home?

Messenger

Your ankles will be my witness
That you would not have lived.

Oedipus

Why do you talk
Of that? The pain is forgotten!

Messenger

Your feet were pierced
And clamped together. I set you free.

Oedipus

The child

In the cradle had a scar—I still carry
The shame of it.

Messenger

You were named in remembrance
Of that scar.

Oedipus

In heaven's name, who did this?
My mother? My father?

Messenger

I do not know. The man
Who gave you to me knows more of the truth.

Oedipus

But you said you found me! Then it was not true . . .
You had me from someone else?

Messenger

Yes, another
Shepherd gave me the child.

Oedipus

Who? Can you
Describe him?

Messenger

They said he was a servant of Laius.

Oedipus

Laius, who was once king of Thebes?

Messenger

Yes,
This man was one of his shepherds.

Oedipus

Is he still
Alive; could I see him?

Messenger

Your people here
Will know that best.

Oedipus

Do any of you,
My friends, know the shepherd he means? Has he
Been seen in the fields, or in the palace? Tell me,
Now! It is time these things were known!

Chorus

I think
He must be the man you were searching for, the one

Who left the palace after Laius was killed.
But Jocasta will know as well as I.

Oedipus
My wife, you remember the man we sent for a little
Time ago? Is he the one this person means?

Jocasta
Perhaps . . . But why should he . . . Think nothing of this!
Do not idle with memories and stories. . . .

Oedipus
No, I have been given these signs, and I must
Follow them, until I know who gave me birth.

Jocasta
No! Give up this search! I am tortured and sick
Enough. By the love of heaven, if you value life . . .

Oedipus
Courage! You are still a queen, though I discover
That I am three times three generations a slave.

Jocasta
No, listen to me, I implore you! You must stop!

Oedipus
I cannot listen when you tell me to ignore the truth.

Jocasta
But I know the truth, and I only ask you to save
Yourself.

Oedipus
I have always hated that way to safety!

Jocasta
But evil lies in wait for you. . . . Oh, do not let him
Find the truth!

Oedipus
Bring this shepherd to me,
And let her gloat over the riches of her ancestry.

Jocasta
My poor child! Those are the only words
I shall ever have for you. . . . I can speak no others!

[*Exit* JOCASTA

Chorus
What is the torment that drives your queen so wildly
Into the palace, Oedipus? Her silence threatens
A storm. I fear some wrong. . . .

Oedipus

Let the storm
Come if it will. I must know my birth,
I must know it, however humble. Perhaps she,
For she is a queen, and proud, is ashamed
That I was born so meanly. But I consider
Myself a child of Fortune, and while she brings me
Gifts, I shall not lack honor. For she has given me
Life itself; and my cousins, the months, have marked me
Small and great as they marched by. Such
Is my ancestry, and I shall be none other—
And I will know my birth!

Chorus

There are signs
Of what is to come, and we may read them,
Casting our thoughts into the future,
And drawing in new knowledge.
For we have seen how the world goes
And we have seen the laws it obeys.
Cithaeron, mountain of Oedipus, the moon
Will not rise in tomorrow's evening sky
Before our king calls you his true father,
His only nurse and mother—and then
You will have your greatest glory.
You will be honored with dances and choirs
For your gentle kindness to our king—Hail
To the god Apollo! May he be content
With all our words.

Pan walks among the mountains, and one
Of the immortal nymphs could have lain with him;
Who was the goddess who became your
      mother, Oedipus?
Or was she the wife of Apollo, for he loves
The wild meadows and the long grass.
Or was it the prince of Cyllene, Hermes?
Or, Bacchus, whose palace is the mountaintop?
Did he take you as a gift from the nymphs of Helicon,
With whom he plays through all his immortal years?

Oedipus

I never knew the shepherd or encountered him,

My people, but the man I see there must be
The one we have been seeking. His age answers
My riddle for me; it holds as many years
As our messenger's. And now I see that those
Who lead him are my servants. But you have known him
Before, you can tell me whether I am right.

Chorus

Yes, we recognize him—the most faithful
Of Laius' shepherds.

Oedipus

                    And you, Corinthian,
You must tell me first. Is this the man you mean?

Messenger

It is; you see him there.

[*Enter* SHEPHERD.

Oedipus

You, sir, come to me,
Look me in the eyes, and answer all my questions!
Did you once serve Laius?

Shepherd

                    Yes, and I was born
In his palace; I was not brought from another
        country. . . .

Oedipus

Your life? How were you employed?

Shepherd

                                    Most
Of my life I watched his flocks.

Oedipus

                            And where
Was their pasture? They had a favorite meadow?

Shepherd

Sometimes Cithaeron, sometimes the places near.

Oedipus

Do you recognize this man? Did you see
        him on Cithaeron?

Shepherd

Why should anyone go there? Whom do you mean?

Oedipus

Here! Standing beside me. Have you ever met him?

Shepherd

I do not think so. . . . My memory is not quick.

Messenger

We should not wonder at this, your majesty;
But I shall remind him of all he has forgotten.
I know that he remembers when for three
Whole years I used to meet him near Cithaeron,
Six months, from each spring to the rising of the Bear;
I had a single flock and he had two.
Then, in the winters, I would take my sheep to their
pens
While he went to the fields of Laius. . . . Did this
happen?
Have I told it as it happened, or have I not?

Shepherd

The time is long since then . . . yes, it is the truth.

Messenger

Good; now, tell me: you know the child you gave
me . . . ?

Shepherd

What is happening? What do these questions mean?

Messenger

Here is the child, my friend, who was so little then.

Shepherd

Damnation seize you! Can you not keep your secret?

Oedipus

Wait, Shepherd. Do not find fault; as I listened
I found more fault in you than in him.

Shepherd

                            What
Have I done wrong, most mighty king?

Oedipus

                        You will not
Admit the truth about that child.

Shepherd

                      He wastes
His time. He talks, but it is all lies.

Oedipus

When it will please me, you will not speak; but you will
When I make you cry for mercy. . . .

Shepherd

No, my king,
I am an old man—do not hurt me!

Oedipus

[*To* GUARDS] Take his arms and tie them quickly!

Shepherd

But why,
Poor child? What more do you want to know?

Oedipus

You gave
The boy to this Corinthian?

Shepherd

Yes, I did. . . .
And I should have prayed for death that day.

Oedipus

Your prayer will be answered now if you lie to me!

Shepherd

But you will surely kill me if I tell the truth.

Oedipus

He will drive my patience to exhaustion!

Shepherd

No!
I told you now, I did give him the child.

Oedipus

Where did it come from? Your home? Another's?

Shepherd

It was not mine, it was given to me.

Oedipus

By someone
In the city? . . . I want to know the house!

Shepherd

By all that is holy,
No more, your majesty, no more questions!

Oedipus

You die
If I have to ask again!

Shepherd

The child was born
In the palace of King Laius.

Oedipus

By one of his slaves?

Or was it a son of his own blood?
Shepherd
My king,
How shall I tell a story of such horror?
Oedipus
And how shall I hear it? And yet I must, must hear.
Shepherd
The child was called his son. But your queen in
the palace
May tell you the truth of that most surely.
Oedipus
Jocasta gave you the child?
Shepherd
Yes, my king.
Oedipus
Why? What were you to do?
Shepherd
I was to destroy him.
Oedipus
The poor mother asked that?
Shepherd
She was afraid.
A terrible prophecy . . .
Oedipus
What?
Shepherd
There was a story
That he would kill his parents.
Oedipus
Why did you give
The child away to this stranger?
Shepherd
I pitied it,
My lord, and I thought he would take it to the far land
Where he lived. But he saved its life only for
Great sorrows. For if you are the man he says,
You must know your birth was watched by evil powers.
Oedipus
All that was foretold will be made true! Light,
Now turn black and die; I must not look on you!
See, this is what I am; son of parents

I should not have known, I lived with those
I should not have touched, and murdered those
A man must not kill!

[*Exit* OEDIPUS

Chorus

               Every man who has ever lived
Is numbered with the dead; they fought with the world
For happiness, yet all they won
Was a shadow that slipped away to die.
And you, Oedipus, are all those men. I think of the
    power
Which carried you to such victories and such misery
And I know there is no joy or triumph in the world.

Oedipus aimed beyond the reach of man
And fixed with his arrowing mind
Perfection and rich happiness.
The Sphinx's talons were sharp with evil, she spoke in
    the mysteries
Of eternal riddles, and he came to destroy her,
To overcome death, to be a citadel
Of strength in our country.
He was called our king, and was
The greatest noble in great Thebes.
And now his story ends in agony.
Death and madness hunt him,
Destruction and sorrow haunt him.
Now his life turns and brings the reward of his
    greatness. . . .
Glorious Oedipus, son, and then father,
In the same chamber, in the same silent room,
Son and father in the same destruction;
Your marriage was the harvesting of wrong.
How could it hold you where your father lay,
And bear you in such silence for such an end?

Child of Laius, I wish, I wish I had never known you,
For now there is only mourning, sorrow flowing
From our lips.
And yet we must not forget the truth;
If we were given hope and life, it was your work.

[*Enter* SERVANT.

Servant

My lords of Thebes, on whom rest all the honors
Of our country, when you hear what has happened,
When you witness it, how will you bear your grief
In silence? Weep, if you have ever loved
The royal house of Thebes. For I do not think
The great streams of the Phasis or the Ister
Could ever wash these walls to purity. But all
The crimes they hide must glare out to the light,
Crimes deliberate and considered. The sorrows
We choose ourselves bring the fiercest pain!

Chorus

We have seen great wrongs already, and they
     were frightening.
Do you bring new disasters?

Servant

                              I bring a message
That I may tell, and you may hear, in a few
Swift words. Jocasta is dead.

Chorus

Then she died in grief. What caused her death?

Servant

It was her own will. Of that terrible act
The worst must remain untold, for I did not watch it.
Yet you will hear what happened to our poor queen
As far as memory guides me. When she went
Into the domed hall of the palace, whirled
On the torrent of her grief, she ran straight
To her marriage chamber, both hands clutched at her
     hair,
Tearing like claws. Inside, she crashed shut the door
And shrieked the name Laius, Laius who died
So long ago. She talked to herself of the son
She once bore, and of Laius murdered by that son;
Of the mother who was left a widow, and became
Wife and mother again in shame and sorrow.
She wept for her marriage, in which her husband gave
To her a husband, and her children, children.
How her death followed I cannot tell you. . . .
We heard a shout, and now Oedipus blazed

And thundered through the door. I could not see
How her sorrow ended, because he was there,
Circling in great mad strides, and we watched
Him. He went round begging to each
Of us; he asked for a sword, he asked to go
To his wife who was more than a wife, to his mother
      in whom
His birth and his children's birth, like two harvests
From the same field, had been sown and gathered.
      His grief
Was a raging madness, and some power must have
      guided him—
It was none of us who were standing there. He gave
A cry full of fear and anguish, then, as if
A ghost was leading him, he leaped against the double
Doors of Jocasta's room. The hinges tilted
Full out of their sockets, and shattered inside
The chamber—and there we saw his wife, hanging
By her throat in the grip of a tall rope. And when
He saw her, he shrieked like a wounded beast, wrenched
      loose
The knot that held her, and laid her on the ground.
What followed was terrible to watch. He ripped
The gold-worked brooches from her robes—she wore
      them
As jewels—and raised them above his head. Then he
      plunged them
Deep into the sockets of his eyes, shouting
That he would never look upon the wrongs
He had committed and had suffered. Now
In his blackness he must see such shapes as he deserved
And never look on those he loved. Repeating
This like a chant, he lifted his hands and stabbed
His eyes, again and again. We saw his eyeballs
Fill with tears of blood that dyed his cheeks,
And a red stream pouring from his veins, dark
As the blood of life, thick as storming hail.
Yes, this is a storm that has broken, a storm
That holds the queen and the king in its embrace.
They were rich and fortunate, and they were so
As we should wish to be. Now, in one day,

See how we must mourn them. The blind rush
To death, the shame, all the evils that we
Have names for—they have escaped none!

Chorus

Has our poor king found ease for his sorrow yet?

Servant

He shouts at us to open the doors and show
To all Thebes the murderer of his father
And his mother's . . . his words are blasphemous,
I dare not speak them. . . . He will be driven
    from Thebes,
Will not stay beneath this curse that he called upon
Himself. Yet he needs help and a guide. No one
Could bear that agony. . . . But he comes himself to
    show you;
The great doors of the palace open, and what you will
    see
Will turn you away in horror—yet will ask for pity.

[*Enter* OEDIPUS.

Chorus

This suffering turns a face of terror to the world.
There is no story told, no knowledge born
That tells of greater sorrow.
Madness came striding upon you, Oedipus,
The black, annihilating power that broods
And waits in the hand of time. . . .
I cannot look!
We have much to ask and learn and see.
But you blind us with an icy sword of terror.

Oedipus

Where will you send this wreckage and despair of man?
Where will my voice be heard, like the wind
    drifting emptily
On the air. Oh you powers, why do you drive me on?

Chorus

They drive you to the place of horror,
That only the blind may see,
And only the dead hear of.

Oedipus

Here in my cloud of darkness there is no escape,
A cloud, thick in my soul, and there it dumbly clings;

That cloud is my own spirit
That now wins its fiercest battle and turns back
To trample me. . . . The memory of evil can tear
Like goads of molten fire, and go deep,
Infinity could not be so deep.

Chorus

More than mortal in your acts of evil.
More than mortal in your suffering, Oedipus.

Oedipus

You are my last friend, my only help; you have
Waited for me, and will care for the eyeless body
Of Oedipus. I know you are there . . . I know . . .
Through this darkness I can hear your voice.

Chorus

Oedipus, all that you do
Makes us draw back in fear. How could you take
Such vivid vengeance on your eyes? What power lashed
    you on?

Oedipus

Apollo, my lords, Apollo sent this evil on me.
I was the murderer; I struck the blow. Why should I
Keep my sight? If I had eyes, what could delight them?

Chorus

It is so; it is as you say.

Oedipus

No, I can look on nothing. . . .
And I can love nothing—for love has lost
Its sweetness, I can hear no voice—for words
Are sour with hate. . . . Take stones and beat me
From your country. I am the living curse, the source
Of sickness and death!

Chorus

Your own mind, reaching after the secrets
Of the gods, condemned you to your fate.
If only you had never come to Thebes . . .

Oedipus

But when my feet were ground by iron teeth
That bolted me in the meadow grass,
A man set me free and ransomed me from death.
May hell curse him for that murderous kindness!
I should have died then

And never drawn this sorrow on those I love
And on myself . . .
Chorus
Our prayers echo yours.
Oedipus
Nor killed my father,
Nor led my mother to the room where she gave me life.
But now the gods desert me, for I am
Born of impurity, and my blood
Mingles with those who gave me birth.
If evil can grow with time to be a giant
That masters and usurps our world,
That evil lords its way through Oedipus.
Chorus
How can we say that you have acted wisely?
Is death not better than a life in blindness?
Oedipus
Do not teach me that this punishment is wrong—
I will have no advisers to tell me it is wrong!
Why choke my breath and go among the dead
If I keep my eyes? For there I know I could not
Look upon my father or my poor mother. . . .
My crimes have been too great for such a death.
Or should I love my sight because it let me
See my children? No, for then I would
Remember who their father was. My eyes
Would never let me love them, nor my city,
Nor my towers, nor the sacred images
Of gods. I was the noblest lord in Thebes,
But I have stripped myself of Thebes, and become
The owner of all miseries. For I commanded
My people to drive out the unclean thing, the man
Heaven had shown to be impure in the house
Of Laius.
I found such corruption in me—could I see
My people and not turn blind for shame? . . .
My ears are a spring, and send a river
Of sound through me; if I could have dammed that river
I would have made my poor body into a bolted prison
In which there would be neither light nor sound.
Peace can only come if we shut the mind

Away from the sorrow in the world outside.
Cithaeron, why did you let me live? Why
Did you not kill me as I lay there? I would
Have been forgotten, and never revealed the secret
Of my birth. Polybus, Corinth, the palace
They told me was my father's, you watched over
My youth, but beneath that youth's nobility lay
Corruption—you see it in my acts, in my blood!
There are three roads, a hidden valley, trees,
And a narrow place where the roads meet—they
Drink my blood, the blood I draw from my father—
Do they remember me, do they remember what I did?
Do they know what next I did? ... The room, the
    marriage
Room—it was there I was given life, and now
It is there I give the same life to my children.
The blood of brothers, fathers, sons, the race
Of daughters, wives, mothers, all the blackest
Shame a man may commit. ... But I must not name
Such ugly crimes. Oh, you heavens, take me
From the world and hide me, drown me in oceans
Where I can be seen no more! Come, do not fear
To touch a single unhappy man. Yes, a man,
No more. Be brave, for my sufferings can fall to no one
But myself to bear!

Chorus
                Oedipus, Creon came
While you were praying; he brings advice and help.
You can protect us no more, and we turn to him.

Oedipus
What can I say to Creon? I have given him
No cause to trust me or to listen. In all I said
Before, he has seen that I was wrong.

[*Enter* CREON *with* ANTIGONE *and* ISMENE.

Creon
I have not come scorning or insulting you, Oedipus,
For those wrongs. [*To servants*] Have you no
    shame before
Your countrymen? At least show reverence to the sun's
Flame that sends us life, and do not let
This curse lie open to disfigure heaven.

Neither earth, nor the pure falling rain, nor light
May come near it. Take him to the palace now!
When evil grows in the family, only the family
May hear of it and look without pollution.

Oedipus

Creon, I thought . . . but now you have struck
    those fears
Away—you will be a gentle king.
But I ask one thing, and I ask it to help you,
Not myself, for I am hated by powers too strong
For us.

Creon

What do you ask so eagerly?

Oedipus

Banish me from the country now. I must go
Where no one can see or welcome me again.

Creon

I would have done so, Oedipus, but first
I must know from Apollo what he commands.

Oedipus

But we have heard all his answer—destroy the
Parricide, the unholiness, destroy me!

Creon

So it was said. . . . And yet we are in such danger;
It is better to hear what we must do.

Oedipus

                                    Why need you
Go to Delphi for my poor body?

Creon

Delphi will never deceive us; you know it speaks
The truth.

Oedipus

                But Creon, I command you! . . . I will kneel
And pray to you . . . Bury my queen as you wish
In her royal tomb; she is your sister
And it is her right. But as for myself, I
Must never think of entering my father's city
Again, so long as its people live. Let me
Have no home but the mountains, where the hill
They call Cithaeron, my Cithaeron, stands.
There my mother and my father, while

They lived, decreed I should have my grave.
My death will be a gift from them, for they
Have destroyed me. . . . And yet I know that sickness
Cannot break in and take my life, nothing
May touch me. I am sure of this, for each moment
Is a death, and I am kept alive only
For the final punishment. . . . But let it go,
Let it go, I do not care what is done with me.
Creon, my sons will ask nothing more from you;
They are men, wherever they go they will take what they
        need
From life. But pity my two daughters, who will have
No love. All that was owned by me, they shared,
And when I banqueted, they were always beside me.
You must become their father. . . . But let me touch them
And talk to them of our sorrows. Come, my lord,
Come, my noble kinsman, let me feel them
In my arms and believe they are as much my own
As when I saw . . . I cannot think. . . . Their weeping,
Their dear voices are near. Creon has pited me
And given me my children. Is this true?

Creon

I sent for them; I know what joy they would give you
And how you loved them once. Yes, it is true.

Oedipus

May heaven bless your life, and may the power
Watching us, guard you more safely on the throne
Than me. My children, where are you? Come near, come
To my hands; they are your brother's hands and they
Went searching out and took your father's seeing
Eyes to darkness. I did not know my children,
And did not ask, but now the world may see
That I gave you life from the source that gave me mine.
Why is there no light? I cannot see you! . . . And tears
Come when I think of the years you will have to live
In a cruel world. In the city they will shun you,
Fear your presence; when they feast and dance in
        the streets
You will not be allowed to watch, and they
Will send you weeping home. And when you come
To the years of marriage, children, who will there be

So careless of his pride as to accept the shame
That glares on my birth and on yours? "Your father
Killed his father!" "Your father gave life where he
Was given life, you are children where he was once
A child." That will be your humiliation!
And who will wed you?
No one, my daughters, there will be no one, and I see
You must pine to death in lonely childlessness.
Creon, you are their father, you alone.
For they have lost their parents. Do not let them go
Into beggary and solitude—their blood is yours.
I have nothing, but do not afflict them with
My poverty. Have pity on them. See, so young
And robbed of all except your kindliness.
Touch me once, my lord, and give your consent.
My children, I would have said much to comfort
And advise you—but how could you understand?
But pray, you must pray to live as the world allows
And find a better life than the father whom you follow.

Creon

No more now. Go inside the palace.

Oedipus

It is hard, but I must obey.

Creon

                       All things are healed
By time.

Oedipus

But Creon, I demand one thing before
I go.

Creon

What do you demand?

Oedipus

                       Banishment!

Creon

Only heaven can answer your prayer. When Apollo ...

Oedipus

But Apollo can only detest me.

Creon

Then your prayer will be
The sooner heard.

Oedipus

You mean what you say?

Creon

I cannot
Promise, when I see nothing certain.

Oedipus

Now!
Exile me now!

Creon

Go then, and leave your children.

Oedipus

You must not take them from me!

Creon

You give
Commands as if you were king. You must remember
Your rule is over, and it could not save your life.

Chorus

Men of Thebes, look at the king who ruled
Your country; there is Oedipus.
He knew how to answer the mystery
Of evil in the Sphinx, and was our greatest lord.
We saw him move the world with his will, and
    we envied him.
But look, the storm destroys him, the sea
Has come to defeat him.
Remember that death alone can end all suffering;
Go towards death, and ask for no greater
Happiness than a life
In which there has been no anger and no pain.

—Tranlated by Kenneth Cavander

Electra

Characters   *Paidagogos*

                    Orestes

                    Electra

                    Chrysothemis

                    Clytemnestra

                    Aegisthos

                    Chorus of Mycenaean Women

Mycenae, before the palace of AGAMEMNON.
[*Dawn.* ORESTES, *the* PAIDAGOGOS, *and* PYLADES *are discovered.*

Paidagogos
  Child of that chief who led the army once in Troy,
  Son of Agamemnon, here before you lies
  For you to see, what you have longed to see.
  It is the ancient and beloved Argos,
  Refuge of Inachos' tormented daughter,
  Apollo the Wolfgod's forum. On that side
  Hera's familiar altar, and just before you
  Golden Mycenae you may see, Orestes,
  And that same murderous House of Pelops, whence
  Your sister snatched you from your father's killers,
  And brought you to me to guard, till you reached
      the age
  When you could avenge that father's murder.

  But now, Orestes, and you Pylades,
  We must decide at once what's to be done.
  The sunlight already bright about us
  Has started the early voices of the birds,
  And the dark sky of stars has faded.
  Before someone emerges from the house,
  Come, lay your plans; this is no time to pause,
  For you are on the verge of deeds.
Orestes
  Old friend,
  How plainly you show your loyalty to me!
  Even in these perils
  You urge us on, and lead the way yourself.
  I shall explain the plan. Listen acutely

And make corrections if I miss the mark.
When I resorted to the Pythian seer
To learn how I might best avenge my father
Upon his killers, Apollo answered,
With neither shield nor army, secretly
Your own just hand shall deal them their due pay.
With this advice in mind, friend, slip into the house
When you can find an opportunity;
See what goes on, then come report to us.
They won't suspect you; with the changes of time
You'll pass unknown. Tell some such tale as this:
You are a Phocian sent by Phanteus,
For he you know is their greatest ally.
Tell them on oath that you come to report
Orestes' death in a fatal accident;
Thrown, say, from his speeding chariot
At the Pythian Games: have this your story.
We meanwhile shall adorn my father's tomb
With our shorn hair and our wine offerings,
As Apollo ordered. We shall return
With that funeral urn we hid in the thicket,
A proof for them of the sweet tale we bring.
That I am already dust and ashes!
What harm is there for me in my rumored death
When I am alive in deed and gaining fame?

But you fathergods, and gods of the country:
O House of my Fathers, on these new paths
Receive me kindly! At the god's urging,
With justice, I come to purify you.
May this land not reject me in dishonor,
But take me in, to make it flourish again.

We have said enough. You go at once, old friend,
And do as I explained. We shall depart,
Obeying Time, which rules all difficult deeds.
[*Wail inside the palace.*

Paidagogos
I thought I heard a servant cry indoors.

Orestes

    The wretched Electra, can it be?
    Shall we wait to hear what she is wailing?

Paidagogos

    No. Not till we try to do as the god said,
    And pour our lustral offerings to your father.
    We must start with that, for that will give us
    Control and victory in the present action.

[*Exeunt* ORESTES, PYLADES *and the* PAIDAGOGOS. *Enter*
   ELECTRA *from the palace.*

Electra

    O daylight,
    O air, the sheath of earth,
    How you have shaken with mourning,
    And you have felt
    The breast beaten for grief
    At the hour of night's going.
    Ah, it is with shame I lie
    In that house, mourning all night
    My father's wretched death.
    No far-off wargod killed him,
    My mother with her lover, with
    Cruel Aegisthos, axe to oak,
    Brought down his head.
    In your house no wailing
    But mine, Father,
    For such perishing.

    But I will not stop wailing
    While I can see the stars glittering,
    Or this day.
    So a bird cries with her young lost,
    And I scream at my father's doors.
    O dark House, Persephone's,
    O earthy Hermes, and you grave
    Furies, you are aware
    Of murders and adulteries.
    Come! Help! Avenge
    My father's murder!
    Send me my brother!
    I begin to sink

Under my trouble.

[*Enter the* CHORUS *of Mycenaean women. Here begins the Kommos, or lament sung by actor and chorus.*

Chorus

Ah Electra, child. Child
Of godless mother. Will you
Still waste for Agamemnon, long since
Guile-snared by that mother, by her delivered
Into the hand of the killer? So may she be
To death delivered. This I dare to pray.

Electra

Gentle women,
You come to comfort me.
This I know, but I can never,
But I will never
Stop mourning my father dead.
You, in your love,
Abandon me to grief,
Only this I crave.

Chorus

But you shall never bring him back with
Prayers and weeping from
The common marsh of death: but in that helpless grief
You waste away, your evils are
Unsolved in these tears.
Why then do you feed your misery?

Electra

Those heads are weak that cannot hold
The death of parents.
But I have set my heart
With that bewildered bird who tells the god,
Crying *Ityn, Ityn* all night. Ah Niobe,
Unfortunate you are, yet blessed
To weep in stone.

Chorus

But you are not alone unlucky
Among mortals, child: your kin
Chrysothemis and
Iphianassa are so, and that one
Whose youth is hidden, whose sufferings covered, whom
The Mycenean land is to receive,

When the god sends him, as
The King: Orestes.

Electra

Him I expect without rest,
Being unwed and childless,
Having my grief, and a fruitlessly evil lot.
Whatever he hears he forgets, or else
Why should he not come as he says?
He longs to, but his longings fall short.

Chorus

Take heart, child, take heart.
Still in the sky
Great Zeus sees everything, and rules.
Give over your anger to him,
Neither forgetting, nor hating too much.
Time is an easy god:
Here by the pasture,
Here by the beach of Krisa,
Agamemnon's child will not be iron forever;
No more will the god who rules by Acheron.

Electra

But most of life has slipped by,
And will not come to me again.
As one whom no parents bore,
One whom no man cherishes,
As a stranger and a beggar in my father's house,
Meanly clothed:
So I wait here by the empty board.

Chorus

With a terrible cry,
Agamemnon met
The murdering edge
In his own bed.
Figure of horror, the issue
Of pleasure and slyness, whether
Some god or a mortal the maker.

Electra

That was my bitterest day: that night
The unspeakable supper was like death for me:
Feast when my father perished at the hands
That were to take my life away.

For them, O god, provide your punishments,
Never enjoyment of their work's fruits.

Chorus

Stop. Stop speaking so.
Can you not think how you distract yourself,
Make yourself pitifully fail?
You increase your troubles when you breed
War in your gloomy soul;
There's no fighting the strong.

Electra

I know I am horror-forced,
And anger will not let me go.
But I will not hold back
So long as I live.
Ah kindly women, from whom shall I hear ever
The good word in season?
Leave me, friends,
Call this trouble issueless.
So shall I hold my lamentations ceaselessly.

Leader

I speak in kindness, as a faithful mother:
Do not feed your frenzy.

Electra

But where is the end of this evil?
Where do they dare to forget the dead,
Among what peoples? There may I be
Unhonored. Or if I ever wed good fortune,
Nesting in peace, still may I never fold
The sharp wings of the wailing due my father.
If the dead are dust and nothing,
If they lie disregarded,
If they are never given
Their due for murder,
Then fear and piety are utterly gone
From among us mortals

Leader

I came for your sake as well as mine, my child.
If my words are wrong, do as you wish,
I follow you still.

Electra

My friends, I am ashamed, you think I mourn too much.

But bear with me, since I have no choice;
What alternative for one who sees the evil?
And I see it, night and day I see it,
Not diminishing, growing. My own mother
Hates me, I live with my father's killers
And obey them; from them I receive the means of life,
Or perish. And that life: do you suppose
It is sweet to me to have to see Aegisthos
In my father's seat, wearing my father's clothes,
Pouring libations at the hearth
Where he brought my father down? When I see
The final insolence accomplished: in my mother's bed
(If I must call her mother) my father's killer?
And she is so calloused, so hardened
With the disease itself, that she fears nothing.
Now she celebrates her work, remembers
The day of the month when with guile she killed him,
To offer the housegods sacrifice and dance.
But I, watching, keep under cover,
Bewail the bitter feast day of my father.
Yet I cannot wail as I would, for she
Attacks me: "Ungodly, ugly girl!
Are you the only one whose father died,
The only miserable mortal? May you sink to Hell,
And the gods of Hell not stop your wailing!"
So she screams till she hears that Orestes is coming.
Then she will shout in my ear, "Did you do this?
Is this your work, you who stole Orestes from me?
But you shall pay for everything!"
So she screams, and behind her, egging her on,
Her lover, that illustrious weakling,
That loud talker, that female fighter!
But I, waiting for Orestes to bring relief,
I begin to fail. He drains my hope,
My hope of hope, with his delaying.
Here is neither wisdom nor piety, my friends,
But evils, which force me to evil.

Leader

Tell me, is Aegisthos near? Or has he left the house?

Electra

He has left, of course. How should I be out,

If he were near?

Leader

If he is away, then,
I may speak further with you?

Electra

Yes, you may speak.

Leader

Let me enquire about your brother.
Is he coming? Delaying? I must know.

Electra

He says he is coming but does not come.

Leader

A man with a great work likes to delay.

Electra

When I saved him I did not delay.

Leader

Take courage. He is the man to help those he loves.

Electra

I trust him, or I should not still be alive.

Leader

Hush for now, hush.
Chrysothemis is at the door, your own sister.
She is bringing offerings for the gods of the dead.

[*Enter* CHRYSOTHEMIS *with offerings. She comes from the palace.*

Chrysothemis

Sister, what are you proclaiming out here at the door?
Won't you learn, after all this time,
Not to pamper a helpless anger?
And you must know that I too suffer
And that if I had the strength
I too should show them what I think of them.
But in foul weather I lower my sails,
I never threaten when I am helpless.
If you would only do the same! . . . Well,
What I say is immoral, of course,
And you are right. And yet, if I am to breathe freely,
I must listen to what they say.

Electra

Horrible; the own child of such a father
And you forget him for that mother!

Your moralizing of course is from her,
None of it yours. Well, choose: either be foolish,
Or else be very prudent, and forget
Those who have been dear to you. Consider:
You say you'd show your hatred if you had the strength,
But you give me no help, though I am given
Completely to the cause of vengeance; you dissuade
    me even.
So we must be cowards too in our misery?
But tell me, what should I gain by silence?
Or I'll tell you. Have I life now? Little;
And yet enough, for I harrow them
To the honor of the dead, if the dead know honor;
While you are a hater in word only,
Living in deed with your father's killers.
I would not yield so—
If they offered me everything that you enjoy,
I would not so yield. For you,
Let the tables of life be richly spread.
Let them overflow. For my sole pasturage
I would be unoffending, I do not crave
Your honors—nor would you, if you were wise.
You might have been your father's: be your mother's:
Belong to her who everyone knows is evil,
The betrayer of your dying father and your own kin!

Leader

By the fear of the gods, no anger!
If you will learn from her, and she from you,
You may still profit from these words.

Chrysothemis

I am accustomed to what she says, my friends,
And I should never have approached her now,
Had I not heard of a greater misfortune coming
To end her mourning.

Electra

What? Tell me of a greater
And I say no more.

Chrysothemis

I'll tell you all I heard.
Unless you stop wailing, they will send you in
Where you cannot see the light of the sun:

Far away and under a low roof
You shall sing your sorrows. Think, therefore;
Do not blame me later, when you suffer,
But think in time.

Electra
And this they really plan?

Chrysothemis
At once; as soon as Aegisthos returns.

Electra
Well then, let him come soon.

Chrysothemis
What, are you mad?

Electra
If that's what he intends, let him come soon!

Chrysothemis
To bring you suffering? What are you thinking of?

Electra
Of escaping you all.

Chrysothemis
Your life here
Means nothing to you?

Electra
How beautiful it is!

Chrysothemis
It might have been if you had learned wisdom.

Electra
Teach me no treachery to those I love.

Chrysothemis
I don't. I teach you to yield to the strong.

Electra
Go. Fawn. Fawn on the strong. I cannot.

Chrysothemis
Still, it would be well not to fall through *folly*.

Electra
I will fall—if I must, to honor my father.

Chrysothemis
But you know that our father understands.

Electra
That's what traitors say.

Chrysothemis
Then you will not listen

To what *I* say?

Electra
No. I have my wits still.

Chrysothemis
Then I shall go about my own business.

Electra
Where are you going? For whom are those offerings?

Chrysothemis
My mother sent me with them to our father's grave.

Electra
What, to the grave of her mortal enemy?

Chrysothemis
Of the man she slaughtered, as you like to say.

Electra
From whom or what did that inspiration come?

Chrysothemis
From something she saw in the night, I think.

Electra
O fathergods! Come! Help!

Chrysothemis
Do you take courage
From her fear?

Electra
If you would tell me what she saw,
I should answer that.

Chrysothemis
I know very little to tell.

Electra
But tell me, tell! It is the little things
By which we rise or fall.

Chrysothemis
They say
She saw our father with her in the light of day.
On the hearth he was, planting his sceptre
Which Aegisthos holds now. From that sceptre grew
A swelling branch which brought at last
The whole land of Mycenae under its shadow.
This I heard
From one who heard her tell her dream to the sun.
It is all I know
Except that it was in fear she sent me.

Now, by the gods I beg you, listen! Don't fall
    through folly!
It will be the worse for you if you push me away!

Electra

Sister, let none of these things touch his tomb.
It is against piety, against wisdom,
To offer our father gifts from that woman.
Give them to the wind, or bury them deep in the dust
Where they can never reach our father's bed;
When she is dead, there let her find them.
Only a woman of brass, an iron woman,
Would offer her murder victim gifts.
Do you suppose the dead man would receive
    them gladly?
From her who killed him in dishonor and cruelty,
After mutilation washing the bloodstained head
To cleanse herself of murder? No! Throw them away,
And cut a lock of hair from your head and one
    from mine,
And give him also this poor thing, all I have,
This plain and unembroidered belt; then fall on
    your knees
And pray that a helper may rise for us
Out of the earth, against our enemies: pray
That the young Orestes may come in his strength
To trample them underfoot, so that with fuller hands
    than these
We may make offering. I think, I think
It was he who sent this dream, prophetic of evil.
Therefore help yourself in this, my sister,
And me, and him, the dearest mortal:
Our father lying underground.

Leader

This girl speaks wisely. You, my friend,
If you are prudent, will do as she requests.

Chrysothemis

I will. For it is right to join for action,
Not wrangle back and forth. But in the name of the gods,
Let there be silence among you, friends,
While I make this effort! If my mother hears,

I shall have bitter things to endure.
[*Exit* CHRYSOTHEMIS.
Chorus
If I am not an utterly false diviner
Bereft of mind,
I am inspired
By Dike, bringing justice with power.
She is coming, my child, coming in no long time!
My courage
Rises, when
I hear this dream.
Your father, King of the Greeks, did not forget,
Nor did that double-edged bronze-headed axe
That struck him miserably down to shame.

Comes on many feet the many-handed
Bronze-shod Fury,
Terrible from ambush.
The godless conjunctions of that mating,
Murder-dabbled, have received no blessing.
Therefore never,
Never in vain
Has this sign come,
To the doers and their helpers! Portents for mortals
Are neither in terrible dreams nor in marvels,
If this night vision is not full of boded good.

Ah Pelops! Your ancient
Chariot racing
Has proved unrelenting
To this, our land.
Since Myrtilos was hurled
From his golden car
To an Ocean bed;
Uprooted cruelly, thrown:
Slain with treachery, slain:
Ever,
Ever with us at home
Suffering and shame.
[*Enter* CLYTEMNESTRA *from the palace. She is followed by a
servant girl bearing an offering of fruits.*

Clytemnestra

    I see you have twisted loose again.
    Aegisthos is gone, who always keeps you in
    Where you cannot revile your kin publicly.
    With him away you do not fear me,
    For you have often enough informed the city
    That I was a tyrant, lost to all justice,
    Outraging you and yours. But it is not I
    Who am insolent, I only answer you.
    Your father, only he, has been your pretext,
    Because I killed him. I killed him: quite clearly
    I say this, for I cannot deny it.
    But Justice seized him also, not I alone;
    And you would have helped too, had you been wise.
    Because that man who you still cry for
    Was the one Greek who could bear to sacrifice
    Your sister. He had not suffered as I had;
    He sowed her, and I bore her. So be it.
    But tell me why, tell me for whom, he killed her?
    For the Argives, you say? But for them
    He had no right to offer up my child.
    Or was it for his brother Menelaos
    My child was slain, and I am not to claim justice?
    Did he not himself have two children,
    Who rather should have died, since for *their*
        parents' sake
    That voyage was undertaken?
    Or had the world of the dead a special craving
    To feast, not on their child, but on mine only?
    Or did your miserable father lack love
    For my child, while tender to Menelaos'?
    Choice of an evil and foolish father.
    So I believe, and so, though you disagree, I say;
    So the dead girl would say, if she were here.
    I do not grieve for these things done;
    Blame me for them, if you think me wrong
    When you can hold your own judgment even.

Electra

    This time you will not say that it was I
    Who started or probed you for these painful things.
    But if you allow me, I shall speak the truth,

About the dead man and about my sister.

Clytemnestra
    I do allow you. If you had always spoken so
    I could have listened without pain.

Electra
    Then I shall speak. You say you killed my father:
    What word more hideous than that avowal,
    Wherever justice lay? But I shall show
    That you killed against justice, in depraved obedience
    To the man with whom you are united now.

    For what offense did Artemis-who-hunts-to-hounds
    Hold all the winds still, there in Aulis?
    I'll tell you: my father once (or so I heard it),
    Playing within the goddess' sacred grove,
    Startled an antlered deer with dappled skin,
    Boasted that he had killed it.
    At that the maiden Artemis grew angry,
    And held the Greeks back till my father paid,
    With the sacrifice of his child, for her stag.
    Such was the sacrifice: there was no other way
    To loose the fleet, either toward home or Troy.
    And so, against his will, constrained, with pain,
    He gave her up; not for his brother's sake.

    But say I'm wrong and you are right,
    Say he offered her up for Menelaos' sake,
    Must *you* then murder him? And by what law?
    Take care, or in issuing this decree
    You issue yourself remorse and punishment.
    For if a killer merits death,
    You must die next, to satisfy that justice.
    Take care, you offer lies for pretexts.

    And now if you will tell me besides
    Why you accept the shameful fruits of your labors;
    Sleep with the very murderer with whom
    You brought my father down; bear children to him,
    Reject your decent children decently born?
    Must I approve? Or will you say
    That all of this is vengeance for your daughter?

An ugly pretext: because of a daughter
To join with a mortal enemy in marriage!
But there is no convincing you, you only scream
That I am being insolent to my mother.
Tyrant I call you, no less than mother,
For under you and your lover
I live in misery, while your other child, Orestes,
Barely escaped you, and now wastes in exile.
You say I raised him up to plague you;
I did, I would, I will if I can, be sure of that;
And therefore if you wish, you may call me
Foul-mouthed and impious.
For I am close to you, close to your nature.

Leader

I see she breathes anger, and whether she is just,
No more concerns her.

Clytemnestra

Then what attention should she receive,
Attacking her mother, old as she is!
Do you think she would wince from any horror?

Electra

I have not lost all sense of shame,
Though you think so. I understand that I
Am lost, that I am beyond the pale.
But it is your heartlessness that forces me;
Crime is quickly learned from crime.

Clytemnestra

A monstrous nursling! She preaches on me
As her text; on what I do, on what I say!

Electra

It is you who talk. It is your deeds that talk.
Even in my words it is your deeds that talk!

Clytemnestra

Artemis! Queen! Witness! When Aegisthos comes
She shall diminish this impudence!

Electra

Do you see?
Having given me leave to say what I would
She will not listen.

Clytemnestra

And so, though you have had your say,

You will keep me from sacrifice by screaming?

Electra

Go. I invite you. Sacrifice.
Do not blame my tongue, for I say no more.

Clytemnestra

[*To servant with offering of fruits.*

Go, my girl, and take these fruits as offerings
That I may raise a prayer up to the King
And cleanse me of the horrors I contain.

Protecting Phoebos, hear the hid thing I say.
I do not speak among friends,
And it would be wrong to open it to the light
While she is near, or with her murderous voice
She would sow through the city futile words.
Listen so, for so shall I pray.

The spectre that I saw last night, Apollo, King,
In that ambiguous dream:
If it is healthful, then fulfill it; if evil,
Let it turn back against my enemies.
Do not let plotters deprive me of my riches,
But let me live always as I am: in safety:
Having the House of Atreus and the sceptre:
Having the friends who now are near me, having
Those of my children who are not bitter toward me.
Apollo, King: listen graciously;
Grant to all mine all that I beg of you.
Also those other things behind my silence:
I know that you know them, being a god;
Being a child of Zeus you know everything.

[*Enter the* PAIDAGOGOS, *as a traveler.*

Paidagogos

Kind women, may I learn
Whether this is King Aegisthos' house?

Leader

It is; you have guessed rightly.

Paidagogos

And am I right that this is the King's wife?
She seems to be a queen.

Leader

Yes. That is the Queen.

Paidagogos
My greetings, lady. I bring sweet news
To you and to Aegisthos, from a friend.

Clytemnestra
I welcome your words, but must know first who sent you.

Paidagogos
Phanoteus of Phocis, on important matters.

Clytemnestra
What are they, stranger? Speak; for I am sure
That coming from a friend they will be pleasant.

Paidagogos
Orestes is dead, to sum it up briefly.

Electra
a-á a-á! This day I die.

Clytemnestra
What did you say? What did you say? Don't listen to her!

Paidagogos
Orestes is dead, I tell you again.

Electra
a-á a-á! I have ceased to live.

Clytemnestra
You: about your business! And you, friend,
Tell me the truth: how did he die?

Paidagogos
That's what I was sent for, I'll tell you everything.
First of all, you must know he went
To the great Greek festival, the Delphic Games.
And there, to be brief where there is much to tell,
I never knew such power or such a man.
Of all the games the judges heralded
He was acclaimed the victor,
Orestes, the Illustrious,
The son of Agamemnon-great-in-Troy.

Such his beginnings. But when a god lays snares
No man can get away, though he be strong.

And so, one day near sundown,
When the swift chariots gathered for a race,
He too drove in among the thronging wheels:
Ten chariots all together, one from Athens.

At first all went well, but at the seventh circling
The Athenian's hard-mouthed foals bolted:
    swinging round,
Crashed full into the Barcaean car;
And at that accident one after the other
Collided, smashed up together, heaped
The Krisan plain with wreckage of chariots.
But this the sly Athenian saw, made way
For the turbulent wave of racers down the center.
Orestes was last, holding his horses in,
Trusting to the finish.
But when he saw that one competitor ahead,
He screamed to pierce his horses' ears, gave chase;
And so they sped, the yokes just even,
First one, then the other winning by a head.

For the whole course so far unfortunate Orestes
Had driven safely, guided his team aright.
But now he loosed the left-hand rein too far,
Forgetting the goalpost, crashed.
The axle broke and he was thrown
Over the rail and twisted in the reins;
As he struck the ground his team bolted away.
And now the multitude who saw him thrown
Set up a wailing for that youth
Who did such deeds and met such end:
Thrown up, legs first, then dragged along the ground,
Till the other drivers brought his horses to a stop,
And freed the bleeding body which his friends
Could recognize no more.
The Phocians burnt it on a pyre,
And in a little urn their envoys bring
The giant corpse, now paltry dust,
To find a grave here in its native earth.

Such is my tale to you, even in words painful,
But for those who watched, for those who saw
As I saw, with my eyes, the greatest horror.

Leader

    a-á! a-á! It seems our master's tree
    Is withered to the root.

Clytemnestra
O Zeus, these tidings:
Joyful, shall I call them,
Or terrible but advantageous?
It is my misery to save my life
Through the sufferings of my own children.

Paidagogos
Why so disheartened at this news, lady?

Clytemnestra
A terrible thing, child bearing.
Though a mother suffer hate, she cannot hate her child.

Paidagogos
Then it seems we came to you in vain.

Clytemnestra
Never in vain: How can you say *in vain*
If you have brought trustworthy evidence
Of his death?—who had his life from mine,
His nourishment from my breasts, then fled?
—Forgot me with this land he left; and ever since
Though never seeing me, has named me
His father's killer who must die in horror?
Neither in the nighttime nor in the daytime
Has sweet sleep covered me, but time in minutes has
    passed me
As one on the verge of death.
And now, on this very day, I lose my fear.
Fear of him, and of her too; for she it was
Living here with me, who was the wider wound,
Draining my lifeblood;
And now at last my days are to be free
Both of her and of all her threats!

Electra
Misery. Now, now may I mourn
Your fate, Orestes, for now is added
Your mother's scorn. Is it not well?

Clytemnestra
Not with you; but he is well as he is.

Electra
Listen, fierce spirit, you the newly dead!

Clytemnestra
It listened. And decided well.

Electra

Exult, for now you have reached your happiness.

Clytemnestra

You and Orestes shall not destroy it.

Electra

No, it is we who are destroyed, not you.

Clytemnestra

[*To the* PAIDAGOGOS] Your coming would have been a
    boon indeed
If you had destroyed this screaming mouth.

Paidagogos

Then I may take my leave, if all is well.

Clytemnestra

Not at all, that would be quite unworthy
Both of me and of my friend who sent you:
Come in, come in; leave her outside to wail
Her evils and the evils of her friends.

[CLYTEMNESTRA *and the* PAIDAGOGOS *enter palace.*

Electra

Did you think that she was bitterly mourning
The wretched son who perished so?
No, she vanished with laughter. Misery.
Beloved Orestes, your death destroyed me.
I have lost all heart for my one hope,
That you would return alive someday
To avenge my father and me. Where must I go?
I am alone without you and my father.
I must go back, I must serve
My father's murderers, my sorest
Human affliction. Is it not well with me?
But never, in such time as may be left me,
Will I go in to them. Here by the gate
I will lay my loveless life to dry up.
If any in the house think me offensive
Let him put me to death: death would be grace,
But life is pain, I have no thirst for life.

Chorus

Where are Zeus' lightnings, where is bright Helios
If they watch this and hide it away in silence?

Electra

e e ai ai

Chorus
Child, why do you weep?

Electra
ai ai

Chorus
Sh, not that great wail.

Electra
You crush me.

Chorus
How?

Electra
On those who are surely going down
To the land of death, you place my hope, and so
Drain me the more.

Chorus
I know that King Amphiareus went down
For a woman's golden chain, and now below the ground

Electra
ai ai

Chorus
He rules the dead.

Electra
ai ai

Chorus
Yes, cry, that murderess

Electra
Was murdered

Chorus
Yes.

Electra
I know, I know; appeared an avenger
For that mourner, but I have none, the one
Whisked off, clean gone.

Chorus
You have really found misery

Electra
Misery most familiar,
Accumulating year by year
Stubbornly, on my life.

Chorus
We have seen its tears

Electra
Then do not turn me
Chorus
Where?
Electra
Where no hope is:
Of my brother to help me.
Chorus
His was the fate of all mortals.
Electra
To fall among competing hooves?
To fall, as that wretched one,
Among the furrowing edges?
Chorus
Unthinkable that horror.
Electra
And he in exile lies
Chorus
ai ai
Electra
Without my burying hands,
Without my tears.

[*Enter* CHRYSOTHEMIS.

Chrysothemis
My dearest, I am running to you with joy
Because I have good news, and the cessation
Of all your troubles and misfortunes!
Electra
And how could you have found me any help
For my misfortunes, when there is none to find?
Chrysothemis
Orestes is with us, listen to me!
Here in the flesh, just as you see me now!
Electra
Poor girl, are you mad? Out of your sorrows
And out of my sorrows, you are making jokes.
Chrysothemis
No, by our father's hearth, in all soberness,
I do assure you I know that he is here.
Electra
Poor girl. And from whom can you have heard

This tale of yours? Who is it you trust so?
Chrysothemis
  Myself I trust, and no one else,
  On the clearest evidence of my eyes.
Electra
  Poor girl. What evidence? What did you see
  To make you heat yourself in this crazy fire?
Chrysothemis
  Listen, by the gods, listen! And when you've heard
  What I still have to tell, decide if I am mad.
Electra
  Yes, speak, speak, if it pleases you to speak.
Chrysothemis
  I will, I'll tell you everything I saw.
  As I approached our father's sepulchre
  I saw that from the top of the barrow
  Fresh streams of milk had flowed, and that a wreath
  Of many kinds of flowers crowned the tomb.
  I marveled as I looked, and I peered about
  For fear someone might be approaching me.
  But when I saw that everything was quiet,
  I crept a little closer, and I saw,
  Close to the tomb, a lock of new-cut hair.
  As I looked, there came to me in my sadness
  A familiar image; that sign I saw
  Was from my best-beloved Orestes!
  I took it in my hands, I did not cry out,
  But my eyes, for joy, filled at once with tears.
  I knew at once, just as I know now,
  That this shining thing could only be from him.
  Who else but you or me could have placed it there?
  It was not I who did it, that I know;
  Nor you: how could you, if you cannot leave the house
  Even to offer mourning to the gods?
  Our mother certainly would never wish to,
  And she could never do it and be unseen:
  Orestes it is who made that offering.
  Therefore take courage: even for you
  The god will not decree the same fate forever.
  That fate has been hard so far. But now, at last, the day
  Gives promise of good things beginning!

Electra
How I pity you for your fondness.

Chrysothemis
Why? Is this not good news I bring you?

Electra
You don't know where you are or what it is you believe.

Chrysothemis
Am I not to believe what I plainly see?

Electra
He is dead, poor girl, and from him will come
Nothing to save you. Look no more to him.

Chrysothemis
a-á a-á! From whom did you hear that?

Electra
From one who was with him when he was destroyed.

Chrysothemis
Where is the man? Oh, I am utterly lost.

Electra
In the house gratifying our mother.

Chrysothemis
a-á a-á! And from whom then can have come
All those death-offerings on my father's grave?

Electra
I should think they must have come from one
Who wished to remember dead Orestes kindly.

Chrysothemis
Oh, miserable fool. How joyfully
I ran with those bright tidings, and never knew
My own delusion! But here I find
The old evils still, and new ones too.

Electra
Yes, that is so. If you take my advice
You'll lighten the burden of this suffering.

Chrysothemis
I suppose I am to raise the dead again?

Electra
That's not what I said, I'm not so crazed as that.

Chrysothemis
What do you ask that I am able to do?

Electra
To undertake to do what I advise.

Chrysothemis

    If it promises well, I shall not hold back.

Electra

    You know nothing is achieved without toil.

Chrysothemis

    I know. I am with you while my strength lasts.

Electra

    Then hear what I have decided to do.
    Henceforth, you know, we have with us no friends;
    Death has removed them, and we are left alone.
    As long as I had reports of our brother
    Alive and prospering, I still had hope
    That he would come one day to avenge his father.
    But now that he is gone I turn to you:
    Aegisthos, our father's murderer,
    You, with your sister, unflinchingly must slay.
    So, I hide nothing from you.

    How can you be so cold? What possible hope
    Can you find to stare at? Your lot is wailing
    For your father's vanishing wealth, and wailing
    While you grow old unmarried and unloved.
    You must not hope that you would ever marry,
    That man Aegisthos is not so careless
    As to permit children of ours to grow
    For his own obvious destruction.
    But if you follow the advice I give you,
    You shall show your love for father and brother,
    And so step forth as a free woman
    Prepared for marriage; all men love the strong.
    In the feasts and assemblies of the city
    Everyone shall laud us for our male courage,
    And that name shall not fail us, living or dead.

    My sister, dearest, trust me, join your father,
    Side with your brother, put an end to my sorrows
    And to your own, in the certainty
    That it is shameful for fine beings to live in shame.

Leader

    In these matters forethought is an ally
    Both for the speaker and the listener.

Chrysothemis
　Dear friends, if her forethought hadn't been perverse,
　She would have kept the caution she discarded.

　What were you thinking of, that you could be ready
　For such madness, and ready to ask my help?
　Don't you see? You are a woman, not a man;
　You are not so strong as those inside the house.
　They are growing larger day after day,
　We are diminishing, we cannot thrive.
　Who would expect to grapple such a man
　And then escape unharmed from that folly?
　Take care, ugly though our treatment is now,
　We shall know worse if your words are overheard.
　It would solve nothing for us, do us no good,
　To win a good report by a shameful death.
　Death itself is not hateful, but to need death,
　And not be able to get it, is hateful.
　I beseech you, before we are quite destroyed,
　Before we are rooted out, restrain your anger.
　All you have said I shall hold as though unsaid,
　Coming to nothing. . . . And you, you be
　Reasonable, even now;
　Helpless as you are, yield to the strong.

Leader
　Listen, for us mortals there is no scheme
　To serve us better than foresight and wisdom.

Electra
　This of course is the expected answer;
　I knew you would reject what I told you.
　This work then must be done by me alone.
　I shall never refuse it as fruitless.

Chrysothemis
　a-á a-á
　If only you had been of that same mind
　When our father died, you could have done all this!

Electra
　My mind was the same, my spirit weaker then.

Chrysothemis
　Try to keep your spirit always constant.

Electra
  This advice means that you will not help me.
Chrysothemis
  Your handiwork is likely to end badly.
Electra
  I envy you your wits, your cowardice I hate.
Chrysothemis
  I shall endure it also when you praise me.
Electra
  That you will never have to endure from me.
Chrysothemis
  The future shall decide that.
Electra
  Go: there is no help whatever in you.
Chrysothemis
  There is, but there is no teaching you.
Electra
  Then go to your mother and tell her everything.
Chrysothemis
  No, I don't hate you as much as that.
Electra
  But you plainly force me into dishonor.
Chrysothemis
  Dishonor, no; I am careful for you.
Electra
  Am I to accept your sense of what is right?
Chrysothemis
  When you are wise you shall guide us both.
Electra
  How hideous to speak so well, and wrongly.
Chrysothemis
  You describe your own malady exactly.
Electra
  Why? Don't I seem to you to speak with justice?
Chrysothemis
  There may be mischief even in justice.
Electra
  I cannot decide to live by that rule.
Chrysothemis
  But if you do what you intend, you'll see I'm right.

Electra
 I will do it, and you shan't divert me.
Chrysothemis
 Is this your answer? You won't reconsider?
Electra
 No. Nothing is more hateful than bad advice.
Chrysothemis
 It is as though you did not hear what I say.
Electra
 These things have long been clear to me. Nothing
  has changed.
Chrysothemis
 Then I shall go. You will never endure
 The things I say, nor I the things you do.
Electra
 Yes, go in there; I shall never follow you,
 Not though you come to me begging on your knees.
 This hunt after vanities is mad.
Chrysothemis
 If you think you have all justice with you,
 Continue to think so. When you fall on evil times
 You will accept my words.
[CHRYSOTHEMIS *slowly enters the palace.*
Chorus
 Why, when we see the wise and obedient birds
 Heedful of those who dreamed them and brought
  them to birth,
 Can we not do as much?
 Neither the thunder of God
 Nor His laws in the stars
 Shall be hid too long.
 O subterranean voice, go, cry cruelly to Atreus' dead
  sons mirthless news,

 That their house is sick; their children, in the
  common strife,
 Cannot agree, live out of love, two ways of life;
 That alone Electra
 Betrayed and shaken,
 Like bird complaining,
 Still wails her father.

Death she disregards, she is ready to face it
To snare those furies. What nature so splendid?

None but the lost
Accept imputed shame, or will to live
Without a name, my child.
Therefore you chose the common saeculum of grief,
And through that ugly dearth made your name safe:
Wise, and the best of daughters.

But I would have you live
Above your enemies' wealth, above their power
Higher than you now are lower.
I see that you labor on a road which is
Not easy, though fertile in the deepest verity,
Which you, in your great piety, bring forth.

[*Enter* ORESTES, *as a weary traveler.* PYLADES *follows with
the urn.*

Orestes
Tell me, ladies, have I been rightly guided,
And have I nearly finished my journey?

Leader
What were you seeking? What did you want?

Orestes
I have been seeking a long time for Aegisthos' house.

Leader
You have come to the right place; your guide was right.

Orestes
Then will one of you tell those inside the house
That our long-desired company is come?

Leader
This girl, as the next of kin, must tell them.

Orestes
[*To* ELECTRA] Will you go then, and explain to them that
Certain Phocians, whom Aegisthos expected—

Electra
a-á a-á! Surely you do not bring
Visible proof of the tale we heard?

Orestes
I have not heard your tale. It was old Strophios
Who sent me to bring you news of Orestes.

Electra
> What news, what news, friend? I am seized with dread.

Orestes
> We offer, as you see this narrow urn
> Containing the small vestiges of his death.

Electra
> a-á a-á! Surely my agony
> Lies visible and palpable before me!

Orestes
> If you are wailing for Orestes' death,
> Know that this vessel contains his ashes.

Electra
> Give me the vessel, friend, if it hides him,
> Give it to me to hold it in my hands,
> For I shall mourn myself and all my race,
> Mourning this dust.

Orestes
> [*To* PYLADES] Bring it and give it to her, whoever she is,
> For she asks this with no evil intent,
> But as a friend or a blood relative.

[PYLADES *gives* ELECTRA *the urn.*

Electra
> O ashes of Orestes, best belovèd!
> I have you back now, with hope gone;
> I did not send you forth so.
> Ah, this is nothingness my hands lift up,
> And I sent you from your house all shining!
> I wish my life might have left me, before
> I sent you to a strange land, and with these hands
> Saved you from death; you would have died with him
> And lain in the one grave with your fathers.
> But now, away from home, in another country,
> Far from your sister, miserably you died;
> And I, with these hands of love, could neither
> Wash you nor dress you nor bear the wretched burden
> From the hungry fire.
> You were tended by the hands of strangers at the end,
> And now you come back to me in this little urn.
>
> Ah, the long joyful fruitless care I gave you!
> You were never your mother's, always mine,

Of all in the house I alone was your nurse,
I your sister, none had that name but me.
Now with your death this is all wiped out
In a single day, everything snatched away
As though a storm had passed: our father gone,
I dead in you, you vanished into death,
The hateful laughing: remains for my pleasure
That monstrous mother whom you so often told me
That you would punish, when you came.
But the bitter spirit, yours and mine,
Has utterly bereaved us,
Sent me, instead of the belovèd face,
Dust and a vain shadow.

a-á a-á! Pitiful body! a-á a-á!

You came a hard road, my love, it was my death;
A hard road, my love, my brother.
And now you must receive me under your roof,
Nothing to nothing. I with you down there
For the rest of time. Up here it was with us
Share and share alike; and now I crave to die,
And not to be excluded from your grave.
I do not think the dead have grief or mourning.

Leader
Your father was mortal, Electra; think
Orestes mortal. Do not wail too much,
We all must suffer death.

Orestes
a-á a-á! What to say? Among the helpless words,
Which to choose? But I can no longer keep from words.

Electra
Why do you suffer? Why do you cry out so?

Orestes
Is it you who are Electra?

Electra
Yes, it is I.

Orestes
What a piteous change.

Electra
Surely it is not I who afflict you so?

Orestes
Oh ruined and dishonored being.

Electra
I am as you so cruelly say, my friend.

Orestes
Oh loveless and bitter life!

Electra
Why are you so hurt as you see me?

Orestes
How little I knew my own misfortunes.

Electra
Did something I said reveal them to you?

Orestes
Seeing you so clearly in your suffering.

Electra
Yet what you see is very little.

Orestes
What more painful could there be?

Electra
To share one's life with the killers—

Orestes
Of whom? What evil do you mean?

Electra
Of my father, and to be forced to serve them—

Orestes
Who forces you to that?

Electra
My mother, she is called.

Orestes
How? With violence? Does she persecute you?

Electra
She persecutes me in every way.

Orestes
And no one is helping you or holding her back?

Electra
No. You have given me the dust of my one helper.

Orestes
Poor creature. As I look my pity returns.

Electra
You are the only one who has ever pitied me.

Orestes
I am the only one with the same sorrow.
Electra
What! You can't be some kinsman of ours?
Orestes
I should answer, if these women were on our side.
Electra
They are on our side, take courage and speak.
Orestes
Give back this jar and you shall learn everything.
Electra
My friend, do not force me to that.
Orestes
Do as I say and you shall not go wrong.
Electra
Don't take away the dearest thing I have.
Orestes
It is impossible.
Electra
Ah Orestes, we are forlorn if I may not bury you!
Orestes
Be quiet, you have no right to sorrow.
Electra
No right to sorrow for a dead brother?
Orestes
It is wrong to speak of him so.
Electra
Am I so dishonored by the dead?
Orestes
No one dishonors you.
Electra
Not though I hold here Orestes' body?
Orestes
That is not his body, though meant to be taken for it.
Electra
Then where is my wretched brother's grave?
Orestes
There is none, the living have no grave.
Electra
What do you say, boy?

Orestes
Nothing that is not true.

Electra
He is alive?

Orestes
If I am alive.

Electra
Are you he?

Orestes
Look at this ring of my father's and see if I speak
the truth.

Electra
O sacred day!

Orestes
Sacred day I cry!

Electra
O voice, do I hear you?

Orestes
Ask nowhere else.

Electra
Do I hold you in my arms?

Orestes
As you shall henceforth.

Electra
O dearest friends, women of the city,
Look at this Orestes, who through trickery
Was dead, and now through trickery is saved!

Leader
We see him, child, and in this blessèd issue
The tears of joy are rising in our eyes.

Electra
O son,
Son of the most belovèd,
You came indeed;
You are found, you came, you see what you desired!

Orestes
I am here, but you must be silent.

Electra
Why?

Orestes
Be silent so that none within may hear us.

Electra
No, by the eternal virgin Artemis,
I cannot think them worthy of my fear:
That excessive mass of womenfolk
Forever inside the house!

Orestes
But think, in women also the wargod
Inhabits. You have experience of that.

Electra
a-á a-á!
Clearly you remind me how insoluble,
How unforgettable, is
This evil of ours.

Orestes
I know, I know, but now that the chance invites us,
We must remember the work we have to do.

Electra
O always,
Every moment I have, I would speak out,
And that is just,
For only now am I free to speak.

Orestes
Yes, but you must preserve this freedom.

Electra
How?

Orestes
Do not speak too long when we lack the time.

Electra
But now that you've come,
Who would give up speech for silence?
Now that beyond thought
I see you, beyond hope?

Orestes
You saw me when the god moved me to come.

Electra
Now what you tell me is
More gracious still: if it was indeed a god
Who led you home, divine
I call your coming.

Orestes
I would not restrain your gratitude,

But I am afraid, your too great joy compels me.

Electra

After so long, your belovèd coming!
But now that you have really appeared, do not—

Orestes

Do not do what?

Electra

Do not despoil me,
Do not deprive me of your face and presence.

Orestes

If anyone tried I should be angry.

Electra

You consent?

Orestes

How could I not?

Electra

O my friends, hearing the unhoped for voice,
Neither withholding my passionate joys
Nor pouring them forth in cries
Stand I! . . . Now I have you, now you have come,
Shown me the belovèd face
Which even in evils I shall never lose!

Orestes

Say nothing needless: do not tell me
How evil our mother is, nor how
Aegisthos in the house of our fathers
Drains, exhausts and vainly scatters our substance;
The telling of it would destroy our chances.
But show me what is fitting at this moment;
Where and how, hidden or manifest,
We are to end our enemies' laughter.
And do not let our mother recognize
In your shining face, that we are in the house;
Falsely wail as though your fate were upon you.
When we shall have won, then we shall rejoice,
Then we shall laugh freely.

Electra

What you wish, my brother, I wish also;
All the pleasure I have I owe to you,
And I should not let you suffer a moment
To gain much for myself; that would never be

The way to serve the beneficent spirit.

You know how we stand, of course; you've heard
That Aegisthos is away from the house,
Our mother within. Do not be afraid
That she will see me smiling with pleasure,
My hatred of her is too old for that;
Besides, since seeing you I have been weeping
For joy. How should I stop, since I have seen you come
Both in death and life? You have worked beyond hope,
So that if my father himself came to me alive
I should think it no marvel, but see and believe;
Therefore lead me as you will.
Alone, I should have done one of two things,
Saved myself in the right way, or found the right death.

Orestes

Be still, I hear someone coming in the house.

[*Enter the* PAIDAGOGOS *from the palace.*

Electra

Go in, strangers;
You bring what none in the house will refuse,
Even though receiving it may not be pleasant.

Paidagogos

You are mad!
Don't you care for life, or were you born witless?
Don't you know that you stand, not on the edge,
But in the midst of the most mortal dangers?
If I had not been waiting all this time
Here, by the door, to watch and to report,
Your plan would have been in the house before you!
This however my caution has prevented.
Now that you've finished all you had to say,
All your insatiable shouting for joy,
Go in. Indecision is fatal;
It is essential to finish up.

Orestes

What reception shall I meet when I go in?

Paidagogos

A good one. First of all, no one knows you.

Orestes

You must have reported that I was dead.

Paidagogos
They speak of you as in the world below.

Orestes
Are they glad? Or what do they say?

Paidagogos
I'll tell you at the proper time; meanwhile
Whatever they do, however bad, is good.

Electra
Orestes, tell me, who is this?

Orestes
Don't you understand?

Electra
No, and cannot guess.

Orestes
Don't you know the man to whom you gave me once?

Electra
What man? What do you mean?

Orestes
The man who through your foresight took me to Phocis.

Electra
Is this the one man I could find to trust
When our father was being murdered?

Orestes
Yes. Ask no more.

Electra
O sacred light! How did you come, the one rescuer
Of Agamemnon's house? And was it really you
Who saved this man and me from many horrors?
O hands beloved! O feet come to serve!
How could you be with me so long and be unknown?
Destroy me with words, and keep your sweet
        work hidden?
Hail, Father! Father you are to me! Hail!
You must know that I have hated and loved you
Beyond all mankind, in this single day.

Paidagogos
Enough, I think. The tale of the time between,
In many revolving nights and days
Shall make these things all clear to you, Electra.

Now, you two standing by: now is the time

To act; now Clytemnestra is alone,
None of her men are in the house; but think,
If you delay you will have to fight with them
And many more much cleverer than they.

Orestes

Pylades, our work permits us no more words;
Let us go in at once, but first salute the gods
Who dwell here on the threshold of the house.

[ORESTES, *the* PAIDAGOGOS *and* PYLADES *perform a brief
ceremony of purification and propitiation.*

Electra

O Lord Apollo, hear them graciously,
And hear me too, who came to you so often
To offer you all I had with these hands.
For now, Apollo, Light God, Wolf God, with all I have
I pray, beseech and beg you, be propitious
To us and the things we intend to do;
Show forth the wages which the gods
Will pay to men for their ungodliness.

[*The men enter the palace, followed by* ELECTRA.

Chorus

Look, look where the wargod creeps,
Blood where he breathes and evil fighting.
And now within the house pursuing
Crime, go the inescapable hounds;
Now it will not be long
Till my hovering dream come down.

And now led by the dead
The stealthy helper enters
His father's wealth, his old abode.
Bloodshed is newly whetted in his hand, and Hermes,
Hiding the snare in darkness,
Leads him to his prize without a pause.

[ELECTRA *enters from the palace.*

Electra

Beloved friends, at this very moment
The men are at their work. Be silent.

Chorus

What work, what are they doing?

Electra
She wreathes the burial urn, the men stand close.

Chorus
Why did you come out?

Electra
For fear Aegisthos might come without our knowing.

[*Within the house.*

Clytemnestra
ai ai,
O loveless rooms alive with death!

Electra
A cry inside. Did you hear it, friends?

Chorus
Heard it shivering. It was cruel to hear.

Clytemnestra
ai ai ai ai,
Aegisthos, where are you, say?

Electra
Listen, another wail.

Clytemnestra
Child, child, pity your mother!

Electra
But you did not pity him, nor pity his father.

Chorus
O city, O wretched tribe,
Your familiar horror is fading.

Clytemnestra
ai ai,
I am stricken!

Electra
Strike, if you can, again.

Clytemnestra
ai ai. Again! Again!

Electra
The same for Aegisthos.

Chorus
The prayers are answered, the earth-buried live,
The murderers' blood is seeping down
To the dead who have been thirsty long;

[*The men enter from the palace.*
The men come forth, the purple hand

Drips with the struggle's sacrifice. I have no blame.

Electra

Orestes, how did you fare?

Orestes

Inside there,
Well, if Apollo guided us well.

Electra

Is the woman dead?

Orestes

No longer fear
That your mother's will could humble you again.

Chorus

Stop there, Aegisthos is in plain sight.

Electra

Why don't you go back!

Orestes

Where do you see him?

Electra

Coming from the suburb, full of laughter.

Chorus

Quick! Inside the house! Finish what's well begun!

Orestes

Courage. We shall.

Electra

Then go, go!

Orestes

We are gone.

[*The men slip back into the palace.*

Electra

What's here belongs to me.

Chorus

Tell this man something pleasing in his ear
To rush him into the fatal struggle blind.

[*Enter* AEGISTHOS.

Aegisthos

Does any of you know where the Phocians are
Who they say have brought us news
Of Orestes' death in a chariot wreck?
You. I mean you! Yes you, who were before
So insolent. It is for you, I think,
Who know the most about it, to inform me.

Electra
  I know, how could I not? Or else I were
  Careless of the fate of my dearest kin.

Aegisthos
  Then where can the strangers be? Come, show me.

Electra
  Inside; for they have reached their dear hostess.

Aegisthos
  Did they really report that he was dead?

Electra
  Yes, and not only in words, they showed us proof.

Aegisthos
  Is it where I can see, to make certain?

Electra
  Yes, it is there. An unenviable sight.

Aegisthos
  What you say pleases me more than usual.

Electra
  You shall be pleased, if your pleasure is there.

Aegisthos
  Silence, I ask, and open out the doors.
  Let all Mycenae and all Argos see,
  So that anyone who still vainly hoped
  For that man's return, may see the corpse
  And take the bit without constraint;
  Learn sense before he meets my punishment.

Electra
  This is accomplished in me. In this time
  I have learned this wisdom: yield to the strong.

[*The doors of the palace open, revealing a veiled bier with
the men grouped around it.* AEGISTHOS *approaches.*

Aegisthos
  O Zeus, without envy I see this fallen
  Figure: if this is impious I say nothing.

  Take the veil from the face. It is fitting
  For the kindred and also for me to mourn.

Orestes
  Lift it yourself. It is for you, not me,
  To see what's lying there and kindly greet it.

Aegisthos
You are right. I will. And you go call me
Clytemnestra, if she be in the house.

Orestes
She is very close, don't look away.

Aegisthos
a-á a-á. What do I see?

Orestes
Why are you afraid? Don't you know the face?

Aegisthos
Into whose terrible snares have I fallen!

Orestes
Haven't you learned that the dead you spoke of
    are living?

Aegisthos
a-á a-á. I see your meaning, you, you
Are Orestes, you who are speaking to me!

Orestes
You are a seer who has been deceived.

Aegisthos
I am lost! But let me say a word—

Electra
Don't let him speak and extend his life with words.
What good is a little time to a creature
Who is fatally netted, and must die?
Kill him as quickly as you can, and give him
To the diggers of graves, to bury him
Where we can never see him. That would be
The only expiation of the old wrongs.

Go in at once. The struggle is not in words,
But for your life.

Aegisthos
Why drive me in? If your work is comely,
Why in the dark? Why not out here?

Orestes
Give me no orders. Go in where you killed my father.
It is there that you shall die.

Aegisthos
Must this house witness all Pelops' evils,
Now and to come!

Orestes
Yours it must: that much I can foresee.

Aegisthos
Your foresight did not include your father?

Orestes
You have much to say, we are slow. Go on.

Aegisthos
You lead.

Orestes
You must go first.

Aegisthos
So I won't escape?

Orestes
No, so you may not die as you please.
I must make sure that death is bitter for you.
Justice should always be immediate;
If the law of death after such deeds
Were fixed, they would be few.

[AEGISTHOS, ORESTES, PYLADES, PAIDAGOGOS *and* ELECTRA
*disappear into the palace. Then the doors open, showing
the living and the dead.*

Leader
O Atreus' suffering seed
To freedom barely emerged
Through this struggle realized.

—Translated by Francis Fergusson

 Philoctetes

Characters
  Neoptolemos
  Odysseus
  Sailors
  Philoctetes
  Merchant
  Hercules

The volcanic, uninhabited island of Lemnos, off the coast of Asia Minor. The shore is edged by cliffs, riddled with caves.

[*Enter* ODYSSEUS *and* NEOPTOLEMOS, *with some sailors, from the crew of* NEOPTOLEMOS'S *ship.*

Odysseus
A boulder in the sea, a strip of sand, and you have Lemnos. Unexplored, uninhabited. And this is where I put him, on this beach, ten years ago . . . Orders, Neoptolemos, I obeyed orders. What could we do? His foot was rotten to the bone, oozing poison. Prayers were blasphemy, sacrifices insults, while he lay there, shrieking, screaming. He never stopped—all through the camp you could hear him . . . those sounds . . . ! But why talk of that? There is no room for talk now, we must be quick. I have a plan to catch him, but if he knows I'm here all my thought is wasted—I can't afford that. So listen, your work begins . . . First, find me a cave with two entrances, a cave which gives you the sun all day in winter, or makes a funnel for the breeze to lull you asleep in summer . . . [NEOPTOLEMOS *begins to climb.*] And a little further down to the left you should come to a spring of drinking water—still there . . . ? Go on, closer . . . but keep it quiet! . . . Has he stayed here? Or has he left? . . . When you know, make a signal . . . Then I'll tell you the plan and we can proceed, you and I, with our mission.

Neoptolemos
You said work, Odysseus, but this is easy. Look, here's your cave.

Odysseus
How high? Near the ground? I can't tell from here.

Neoptolemos
Just above me . . . No tracks, though, no sign . . .

Odysseus
Careful! He could be lying there asleep.

Neoptolemos
No, I can see inside. Empty, no one at home.

Odysseus
Has it been lived in? Any food?

Neoptolemos
A pile of dry leaves pressed down to make a bed . . .

Odysseus
But otherwise empty? Nothing on the ground?

Neoptolemos
A cup scooped out of a block of wood. Whoever made it never learned to carve . . . And some pieces of kindling here.

Odysseus
Yes, all his wealth is in this cave.

Neoptolemos
Wait, something else . . . [*He lets out a cry.*] Rags! . . . drying in the sun . . . clotted with matter!

Odysseus
We've found our man. He still lives here. He may be out looking for food, or perhaps he knows of leaves for the poison in his wound—but he must be close. Sick, one limb useless, how could he go far? Send a man to keep watch. [NEOPTOLEMOS *obeys.*] If he comes, I want to be warned. He'd rather lay hands on me than the whole Greek army put together.

Neoptolemos
Someone is going now. He'll guard the path. Next?

Odysseus
Next, my boy, your mission. And I hope I shall see you, the son of Achilles, fulfil this mission in a style worthy of your father. I don't just mean, be brave. I mean, if what I say now is a surprise, something you were not expecting, remember, you are here to assist me, and obey. Obey absolutely.

Neoptolemos
Your orders, sir?

Odysseus

I want Philoctetes. And you must get him for me. You will use words. And with words, steal his soul . . . He will ask you who you are and where you come from. You will say, "Son of Achilles, from Skyros." So far, no deception. *But* . . . you are sailing home, you have left the Greek army which—now remember—which you hate. Hate! The Greeks, you tell him, sent an appeal to you. Come to Troy, they said, you are our one hope of taking the city . . . You went to Troy. But when you asked for Achilles' armor—and you had every right, he was your father—they saw fit to refuse. Instead they handed the armor over to . . . Odysseus. Say what you like about me, make the words cruel, be savage. You won't hurt me. But if you fail, the whole Greek army will be hurt— deeply. We must bring back that bow. Without it there will be no triumph, no victory for you at Troy. Now, Philoctetes would never listen to me, but you he will trust. I'll tell you why. You owe allegiance to no one; no one forced you to come; you were not part of the original expedition—none of which applies to me. If he finds me here, and that bow is in his hands, I die. And since we are together, so will you. Rather than cause your death I have had to plan, contrive. For the sake of that bow, young man, that invincible weapon, you are about to become a thief! . . . I know, I know, Neoptolemos, it isn't your nature. To you lying is wrong, intrigue is wrong. Yes, but victory is sweet—seize it! Dare! Time will put us in the right, you'll see. Today, just for today, forget shame, and serve me. Then for the rest of your life, be as virtuous as you like.

Neoptolemos

Odysseus, there are things—I have only to hear the words and I feel pain; ask me to do them and I rebel. I can't. This is deceit. My whole being shouts no to it. And my father, they tell me, he was the same. I am ready to use force to take this man off Lemnos, but take him by a trick—no! He has one good leg and we number—look, how many? We have the strength, can he resist? I was sent here under your command and I shall be accused of mutiny. I don't enjoy the thought. But if a lie is the only way to succeed, let me fail, sir, and stay honest.

Odysseus

Good. Like your father, your upright, honorable father. And at your age I was the same. Slow with words, quick with action. But now I have experience, and I realize that in life it is not action that counts. Words are what matter; words have the power.

Neoptolemos

Tell a lie. Is that your order or not?

Odysseus

My order is, Bring me Philoctetes by strategy.

Neoptolemos

Why strategy? Why not persuade him?

Odysseus

You'll never persuade him. And you can't take him by force.

Neoptolemos

Why not? What is so terrible about him? Has he no fear, no weakness?

Odysseus

His arrows. They are deadly and they never miss.

Neoptolemos

Then even to go near him is dangerous?

Odysseus

Unless, as I said, you use strategy.

Neoptolemos

You feel no guilt when you tell a lie?

Odysseus

No—suppose the lie saves my life . . .

Neoptolemos

But how does one say the words and not blush?

Odysseus

Think of what you gain and don't be shy. This is no time to be shy.

Neoptolemos

What do I gain if he goes to Troy?

Odysseus

His bow will take the city. Nothing else can.

Neoptolemos
But you all said I was to conquer Troy. Wasn't that true?

Odysseus
It was. And that bow can do nothing without you. But *you* can do nothing without the bow.

Neoptolemos
I see. That is the great prize, then . . .

Odysseus
Do what I ask, and you win two prizes.

Neoptolemos
How do you mean. I may agree, but I must be sure.

Odysseus
Two prizes, Neoptolemos—one for courage and one for brains!

[NEOPTOLEMOS *reflects*.

Neoptolemos
I'll do it . . . and not be ashamed. That's all gone.

Odysseus
You remember my instructions to you . . . ?

Neoptolemos
Yes, yes, I told you, I agree to everything!

Odysseus
You wait and meet Philoctetes here. I'll leave you now, in case I'm seen, and dismiss your sentry back to the ship. If I think you're taking too long I'll send him back, the same man, but disguised as a merchant so that his uniform can't be recognized. He may say some puzzling things, boy, but you improvise, take your cue from him. I'm going back to the ship—you are in charge now . . . May the god Hermes help us, as he helps all conspirators, and the Goddess Athene of victories, who guards my interests day and night.

[*Exit* ODYSSEUS.

Sailors
Here in this strange country of rock and sand and silence
    he'll find us, suspect us.
How do we speak to him?
We must watch every word, tell some things, hide others.
How? Tell us how? You are leader, born to great gifts,
    and great burdens . . .
To see further than other men, to have power, to say

"Now we act! Now this is right!"

You are the son of Achilles, a king's son, you decide,
    you say.

Neoptolemos

If you could search for him . . . no, we must wait. Watching—however hard—is our way now. Hold firm on your
strength. He may seem terrible, when he comes, but
stand, don't flinch. Be beside me—every minute.

Sailors

Every minute. Count on us. We are ready, not one nerve
    here will fail you.

But he may come on us now, as we talk, and we never
    see him.

There are paths and tracks on this island, hollows, ra-
    vines of dry stones,

He may be hidden, waiting,

Or coming now.

Is this his home, does he live here?

Will he return?

Neoptolemos

Yes, he lives in stone, sleeps on rock.

Sailors

His home—a tunnel in the earth.

Where is he?

Neoptolemos

Hunting food. What else can he do? He has his arrows,
they kill for him. One swift blow, and he lives—the only
way he can live. But always, hour by hour, haunting
him—the pain. He can find no cure here, no relief.

Sailors

Pity him, then, pity him.

To wake up in the black night, screaming with pain to
    the stone walls alone,

To drag out days, the disease gorging itself on his life,

Faint in the sun's glare . . .

And still live . . .

How has he endured? How?

Heaven scorns us, breaks us, allows us one, only one,
    right—to suffer.

Once he had a home, a family to love him and be true to
    him, a life of peace . . .

And now he is a beast, struggling with other beasts to
    stay alive, starving,
His one companion, pain—and thoughts . . .
Thoughts that claw at his mind, never resting, never,
    never resting.
He cries out—the mountains hear him, the echoes reply
    to him, mock his torture, eavesdrop on his agony.

Neoptolemos

I believe without question his sufferings have a meaning.
There must be a purpose, an end we do not yet see, because only a higher power can see it. Perhaps this power
is making sure he doesn't turn his invincible weapon
on Troy before a certain time. Many conditions must be
fulfilled before the city can be conquered . . .

Sailors

Wait! Not a sound . . . !

Neoptolemos

What is it?

Sailors

I heard him . . .
A sound like someone in pain . . . from over there . . .
No there, that way . . . surely . . .
It was, I'm certain it was. I heard a voice from the path,
As if something was being dragged, with terrible effort,
    being forced over the ground . . .
The voice was hoarse, I heard the breath rasping,
    sharp . . .
Now, my boy, you must . . .

Neoptolemos

Yes! What . . . ?

Sailors

Take command. At once. The man we came for
    is here . . .
No longer someone out there in the undergrowth, but
    here, here with us . . .
And he isn't singing on a pipe, either, like some shepherd
    in the fields . . .
He's nearer now, he stumbled then . . .
That was the sound, yes, the sound forced out of him . . .
He may have seen our ship . . .
He's trying to shout, make them hear on board . . .

That was loud.
He's close . . .
I'm frightened . . .

[*Enter* PHILOCTETES. *He hails the* SAILORS *with a shout.*

Philoctetes

Strangers! Who are you? What brings you here? Don't
look for harbors, there's no life on this island . . . Have
you come far, from . . . Greece? Your clothes are Greek
and to me they seem the dearest in the world. But I
want to hear you speak . . . No, stay with me, don't be
afraid, nothing can harm you. This loathsome animal is
a man; all he asks is pity. He's suffered much, alone in
this desert, no friends, torment, torment . . . Just speak,
in the name of love, just one word . . . Answer me, at
least! If nothing more, we can talk. Don't deny me that!

Neoptolemos

You ask who we are, stranger. We are Greek.

Philoctetes

The dear, dear sound of a human voice, speaking words
from my own country, after all this time . . . Boy, why
did you come? What do you look for here? Safety?
Peace? Tell me the wind you sailed by—that wind will
be my dearest friend. Tell me who you are, everything,
I must know.

Neoptolemos

I was born on the island of Skyros and there I sail—
home. My name is Neoptolemos, son of Achilles . . . You
know everything.

Philoctetes

Home—to Skyros! And you are the son of my dear friend
Achilles. Where have you come from? What makes you
land here?

Neoptolemos

I am one day's sail out of Troy.

Philoctetes

Troy? But you were not with us when the fleet set out.

Neoptolemos

Were you part of that great expedition?

Philoctetes

Look at me, don't you know me, boy?

Neoptolemos

Know you? But I never saw you till now.

Philoctetes

And you never heard my name, no one told you about my day-by-day extinction here.

Neoptolemos

No, I have heard nothing, nothing of that, believe me.

Philoctetes

No, there will be no end, no hope. I gall heaven. My life here—look at it, and nothing, not a whisper, reached home. No one in all Greece knows. Threw me off their ship—but that crime, that monstrous crime, stays secret. Their mouths are shut, they're safe and well, while my disease blooms in me, gains ground daily . . . Young man, son of Achilles, look, this is the man who was given charge of the weapons of Hercules. Yes, this! You may have heard of me. I am Philoctetes! And here I live, alone, discarded, where the Greek generals and Odysseus left me. My whole body raged with fever, consumed by poison . . . the snake's fang had struck deep and the venom was deadly. The fleet sailed out from Chryse, anchored here. Then they brought me ashore, and left. But I stayed, I stayed, alone and sick! The voyage here had exhausted me and I fell asleep on the shore under that overhanging cliff. They thanked heaven, weighed anchor, and sailed on without me . . . Not without mercy, though. They flung a few rags down beside me, and some scraps of food—pray god they have to exist on as much some day! Imagine, boy, you imagine my awakening then—deserted. I wept. Yes, I shed tears of agony. The fleet, all the ships I brought with me—gone. The island—a wilderness, no hope of rescue, and if the disease overpowered me I would lie where I fell. Everywhere I looked I found despair. Despair—I could have gorged myself on that, oh, yes! . . . The days crawled by, and I existed. There, in that burrow, I eked out a life— I had to. My bow here filled my stomach. There were pigeons flying about and I used to shoot at them. But even then, when my arrow had found its home, I still had to fetch the kill, haul myself along—and the pain in me all the time—dragging my useless, wounded foot behind. And if I needed a drink, or there was frost on the ground and I had to chop wood—and that often happened in the winter—well, I managed. I crept out and I managed. Then my fire would die, and I had to scrape two rocks together to coax out a reluctant spark, just a brief spark, but it was all my life to me. And so you see, I have a roof over my head, I have a fire, I am provided with everything—except a cure! . . . Now, this island. Listen, boy, you should know what kind of place it is. No ship comes near it—not if she's on course. There's no harbor, no trade, no one to make you welcome. No one in his senses makes a voyage here. Sometimes a ship was forced in shore—such things may happen often . . . over the years. But these people, I can tell you, when they come, they say how sorry they are for me, their pity may even extend to a few bites to eat, perhaps clothing, but take me home with them—I only say the words and they lose interest . . . Ten years I've rotted here! Ten years I've starved and suffered so that my disease can grow fat. Now do you see, boy, what the two Greek generals and Odysseus, our great warrior Odysseus, have done to me. May god in heaven punish them with ten such years!

Sailors

You had the pity of those who came before, and you have ours. It is your right, Philoctetes.

Neoptolemos

And I'll be your witness Philoctetes. Every word of that is true. I met the Greek generals and Odysseus. They are criminals.

Philoctetes

So you know them, too. They spread chaos everywhere, those men. And what did they do? You are angry—yes?

Neoptolemos

Oh, let me slake my anger in some action! Then they'll find out in Mycenae, and they'll find out in Sparta, that Skyros too mothers brave men.

Philoctetes

Good, good, my boy. They've earned your hate, then. But how? What have they done to you?

Neoptolemos

I'll tell you, Philoctetes, they . . . I can scarcely say it, the way they dealt with me, the insults, the indignity . . . You see, when, by the will of heaven, my father died . . .

Philoctetes

Wait, before you go on, I want to hear . . . Achilles is dead?

Neoptolemos

No man on this earth killed him. It was said an arrow from the god Apollo ended his life.

Philoctetes

Then the one who killed and the one who died were worthy of each other. You've made it hard for me, boy. I want to hear what happened to you. But my grief for Achilles . . . my friend . . .

Neoptolemos

Grieve for yourself. You have cause. Achilles is far away and dead.

Philoctetes

Yes . . . So, you have been their victim too. Go back over it, tell me what happened.

Neoptolemos

The noble Odysseus came to me, brought ships, armament, a full-scale expedition. He said, true or not—I'll never know, that now my father was dead only I could win the war against Troy. Heaven's will made the task mine. Bringing news like that no one could have held me in Skyros. More than anything else I longed to see my father, just once, before they buried him . . . I never really knew him. And then, to be told I would conquer the fortress of Troy, the glory all be mine . . . I set sail at once! Two days, and my fleet shipped oars at Sigeion . . . Sigeion, the bitter unhappiness of that place! As I walked up the beach the whole army swarmed round to greet me, swearing they saw the dead Achilles alive again . . . And there he lay, my father. I paid my last respects to him, then I went straight to Agamemnon and Menelaus, my friends—or so I thought. I was a fool. I asked them for the armor my father used to wear, his spoils, all his possessions. When I heard their answer my heart sank. "Son of Achilles," they said, "take everything your father owned, no one will stop you. Only, leave his armor. That is in the hands of someone else—Odysseus." My blood caught fire, I was choked with rage. I stood up and shouted at them. "Thieves, how dare you give away my armor, yes, *mine!* without consulting me?" Then Odysseus—he was there, standing beside them— he spoke up. "Come, my boy," he said, "they did right. I was there when Achilles was killed. I earned the armor when I rescued his body." That man infuriated me! I called down every curse I knew upon them for letting Odysseus take my armor. Odysseus had to reply, even the cautious, controlled Odysseus—I had said things that stung him. "You were never one of us," he said, "you stayed away in a place where fighting was not required, you talk too much and too loudly, and when you sail back to Skyros, boy, it will not be with Achilles' armor!" These are the sneers, the insults I had to bear, and so I set sail for home, robbed of my rightful property by Odysseus, the treacherous, blackhearted scum, Odysseus! And yet I blame him less than his commanders. Know a country by its rulers, know an army by its generals. Men learn that right and wrong can be abused only if they are taught so by their masters . . . And that is all my story. But if Agamemnon and Menelaus have an enemy, that man is my friend—and I hope the friend of heaven.

Sailors

I was there, that day, when all the evil force of the generals' spite turned on our leader. I prayed to heaven that day, when they gave his father's armor away. I prayed to the giver of life, the mother of Zeus himself, to the bountiful Earth, who reigns over the mountains and the rich golden streams of the Paktolos. And I call her to witness now, blessed goddess, supreme in power, most high, most awful, ruler of bull-slaying lions—they gave that armor to Odysseus!

Philoctetes

Your grievance wins you all my trust, my faith. Welcome . . . friends! We make a harmony, you and I. They've been at work, I can tell, the two generals, and Odysseus.

I know him so well. His tongue will dabble in any lie, he cannot feel remorse, and when he acts, the end is always evil. But one thing about your story, Neoptolemos, I find hard to believe. Ajax was there and saw it happen, and he did nothing?

Neoptolemos
Ajax was dead, my friend. He would have stopped that piracy if he had been alive.

Philoctetes
What? Ajax gone ... dead ... ?

Neoptolemos
The light of the sun shines on him no more.

Philoctetes
It's wrong, wicked! Agamemnon and Menelaus—their unnecessary lives go on. They are immortal!

Neoptolemos
True. And you know, their power in the Greek army is growing every day.

Philoctetes
There was one good man, an old man—my friend, Nestor. He saw what was happening, and he spoke his mind.

Neoptolemos
This is a bad time for him. His son has been killed. He is quite alone.

Philoctetes
He lived for his son, so two have died. Oh, Neoptolemos, of all men in the world I wish it had not been them. Is there any sense in this—they are dead, Odysseus lives on. It should have been his corpse lying there, but no.

Neoptolemos
Odysseus is clever, he wrestles well with life. But even the clever wrestlers are tripped sometimes, Philoctetes.

Philoctetes
Wait, I must ask you ... Patroklos. Where was he? He was your father's dearest friend.

Neoptolemos
He was killed, too ... War! Listen, I describe war in one sentence. War never killed a single criminal, but it has murdered an army of heroes.

Philoctetes
I know, I've watched it happen. And while we talk of

it tell me about that other useless man, that front-line fighter with his tongue, but clever. What became of him?

Neoptolemos

That describes . . . but you don't mean Odysseus?

Philoctetes

No, no . . . this one was someone called . . . Thersites. When everyone else called for silence, there he was, talking, talking. Is he alive, do you know?

Neoptolemos

I never saw him, but I heard he survived.

Philoctetes

He would. The evil in this world never dies. No, eternal powers lovingly protect it. They snatch all that is foul and corrupt out of danger—I think it's a game for them— then down, down into the grave goes anything fine and good. I can find no meaning in it, nothing to revere. How can I feel reverence for heavenly powers when all I see of them is their crimes?

Neoptolemos

From now on, Philoctetes, I shall survey Troy and the Greek generals from a good safe distance. Where corruption is a lord, where fine things die, where all that is mean and shabby has the power—a world like that I can't love. No, in future, Skyros and its rocks will be enough for me; I am happy there; I am at home . . . I shall go back to my ship now, but I wish you well, Philoctetes, with all my heart. May heaven cure you of your sickness, as you surely wish.

[*To* SAILORS:] We must go. We weigh anchor as soon as we get a following wind.

Philoctetes

You're leaving already, boy?

Neoptolemos

Yes, we must. It's nearly time to sail, and I want to be near my ship.

Philoctetes

Boy—listen—I'm giving you the power of life and death over me! I'm asking you, in the name of your father and your mother, in the name of everything you hold dear at home—don't leave me behind! Don't leave me here alone, in this prison, this hell! . . . You've heard what it's like,

you've seen it. Give me a corner in your ship, anywhere!
It's an ugly sight, I know, an ugly cargo, but try, *try*
to bear that. You're a king's son—honor has a good sound
to you, shame appalls you . . . leave me here and you
earn nothing but disgrace. But just do what I ask and
you'll have honor, honor everywhere, if I reach my home
in Oeta alive. Come, the cost is . . . what? One day's
work—no, not that. Brave it out. You can take me and
throw me where you like—in the prow, in the stern, in
the bilge—wherever I'll be least trouble to your crew
. . . Say yes, boy! In the name of Zeus who pities people
in distress, can't I persuade you? . . . Look . . . [PHI-
LOCTETES *kneels at* NEOPTOLEMOS's *feet*.] . . . this is
what I do, broken in heart and body, lame! Don't abandon me to this desert, this utter loneliness. Save me,
take me to your home—no, as far as the plains of Chalk-
edon in Euboea—from there the journey to my country
is nothing. I'll get back somehow to Trachis and the
Spercheios, and because of you I'll see my father again
. . . and yet, it's ten years and I am afraid for him. Is
he dead by now? When travelers came I sent him
messages, time and time again I begged him to launch
a ship, come himself, and save me. But either he's dead
or . . . I don't know, more likely those messengers had
no time for my petty business and hurried on to their
homes. But now you are my messenger and my rescuer
all in one. I come to you—be the one to save me, the one
to pity me, seeing that man walks in the midst of danger
all his life, threatened with sorrow when he is most
happy . . . If you are free from suffering, then watch.
When your life goes well, then is the time to be on
guard. You may never know the day of your destruction.

Sailors

Listen to him, sir . . .

He deserves pity—you heard what he said . . .

He's suffered terribly, more than any man should
   have to bear . . .

I pray no one I love has to suffer like that.

But if you hate those two generals, sir, listen . . .

What they did was wrong, but we can use it . . .

Now we are here, let us help Philoctetes . . .

We'll put him on board our ship, as he asks...
She's well supplied, she's fast...
Take him back home.
It is his right—
And our duty—
Heaven watches, sir.

Neoptolemos
Be sure. Now you say yes, while it's easy for you. But
when you live with this disease, when it fills every
day—will you stand by what you have just said?

Sailors
Always. You'll never have cause to say we broke our
word. It would be foul, treacherous!

Neoptolemos
We have a friend, and he needs our help. If he thought
I was slower than you to take my share, however hard,
I would feel disgraced. Is it decided? . . . Then we sail.
Quick, we leave now. The ship will carry us all, she
won't refuse. I only pray that heaven guards us on our
voyage out of here, wherever we sail.

Philoctetes
Thank god, thank god in heaven for the dawn of this
day, for your blessed goodness, sir, for your friendship,
all of you—how can I ever show my gratitude, how can I
pay this debt? . . . We must go—no, first, boy, we'll take
a strict and formal leave of my home. Come inside and
see what I call a home, see what I had to live on, then
you'll know the strength of my will. I think the sight
alone would have defeated anyone but me. But I refused
to give way. I learned, I forced myself to learn, how to
make suffering my friend.

Sailors
Wait! Something's happened. Two men—one from our
ship, the other . . . a stranger . . . running . . . Find out
what they want first.

[*Enter one of* NEOPTOLEMOS's *crew, disguised as a* MER-
CHANT, *with another* SAILOR.]

Merchant
Son of Achilles, Neoptolemos, I asked my friend here—
he was guarding your ship along with two others—I
asked him where you might be found. We met, it was

sheer chance, but I happened to put ashore on the same
beach. I'm on business, not a big cargo, you know, on my
way home from Troy to Peparethos—we have vineyards
there—and I heard that those men were all your crew,
so I thought I couldn't set sail again, nothing said,
without telling you my news—and seeing whether it's
worth anything to you. Things are happening, sir, the
Greeks have plans, and they concern you—but you have
heard nothing, I think. No. I said plans, but now they
are more—they are action. No time was wasted . . .

Neoptolemos

I am grateful to you, stranger. You thought of me, and I
would be a hard man if I forgot your kindness. Tell me,
I want to know what the Greeks are doing. You've heard
their latest plans?

Merchant

Yes. A squadron of ships under Phoenix and the sons of
Theseus—they've left already, they're hunting you.

Neoptolemos

They mean to get me back? How? Force—or persuasion?

Merchant

I don't know. I simply tell you what I've heard.

Neoptolemos

And Phoenix leaps to action, launches his fleet, just to
please the Greek generals . . . ?

Merchant

Listen, they are on their way now, not a day was lost!

Neoptolemos

But Odysseus wasn't prepared to carry his own messages.
What held him back? Fear?

Merchant

He set out himself, just as I was leaving, he and Diomedes—after someone else.

Neoptolemos

A visit from Odysseus himself! Whose is the honored one?

Merchant

Someone called . . . [*The* MERCHANT *breaks off and
draws* NEOPTOLEMOS *aside.*] . . . Wait, who is this man
here . . . ? Careful, keep your voice down.

Neoptolemos

This is Philoctetes, friend—you have heard of him?

Merchant

No more questions, sir. Leave now—hurry! Set sail at once and don't be found on this island!

Philoctetes

What's he saying, boy? Why is he whispering? Don't let that merchant strike any bargains over me!

Neoptolemos

I'm not sure yet what he's saying, but I want it said out loud so that we can all hear.

Merchant

Sir, I beg you, sir, don't make trouble for me with the Greek generals. I shouldn't be talking to you like this. I'm a poor man, I have a business, I make a living from supplying the army . . .

Neoptolemos

I am a sworn enemy of Agamemnon and Menelaus. And because he hates them too, this man is my greatest friend. Are you here to help me? . . . Good, then tell me all you've heard, all! Hide nothing.

Merchant

Think what you're doing, boy!

Neoptolemos

I have been thinking, thinking very carefully.

Merchant

I hold you responsible for anything that . . .

Neoptolemos

Do! Now, tell me.

Merchant

I will, then. It's for Philoctetes here that those two I was telling you about—general Diomedes and the mighty Odysseus—have sailed out from Troy. They've taken an oath to bring him back. Either they'll persuade him or . . . well, they have the men, they'll use force. Everyone in the Greek army heard Odysseus say so. He had more confidence then Diomedes, he was the one who believed it could be done.

Neoptolemos

But for ten years this man has been no more to the Greek generals than waste, the garbage of the war, left behind on an island sometime . . . they don't quite remember when. And now—they love him, they long for him. Why? . . . Or is this the power of justice, forcing retribution?

Merchant

This is the story, then. I tell you all, because it will all be new to you. In Troy there was a man called Helenus, he was a prince, the son of Priam—and he had the gift of prophecy. So one night, the man whom everyone calls corrupt, vicious, every kind of foul name—Odysseus —he went out and captured Helenus. Single-handed. Clever of him. He brought back his prisoner, showed him off in the middle of the Greek camp—a great prize, magnificent! Then Helenus began to prophesy. All their future he laid bare, but most important—he said they would never break the resistance of Troy until they persuaded Philoctetes to come away from the island where he lives now. Immediately the prophet had finished, Odysseus undertook to bring back Philoctetes to the Greek army. He hoped, of course, that he would find him willing to be brought back, but even if he was not, Odysseus would still succeed. Anyone who wishes can have the privilege of cutting off his head if he fails. . . . That is all I know, boy, but my advice to you, and him, and anyone you care about, is—hurry!

Philoctetes

No—no! That creature, that vermin, he's sworn, has he, that he'll persuade me back into the Greek army! Oh yes, I'll be persuaded . . . And I'll be persuaded just as easily to climb back out of my grave!

Merchant

That I cannot tell you. I'm going back to my ship. May god keep the rest of you safe and well.

[*Exit* MERCHANT.

Philoctetes

That man, that Odysseus, he makes me gasp. He imagines he'll get me on his ship, then parade me in front of the whole Greek army—all with a few soothing words. No. I'd rather listen to my most cruel enemy, the snake that made my leg here useless. But Odysseus can't relent, he'll hound me to the end. He'll come, I know him. Quick boy, let's put a long stretch of sea between us and Odysseus. Shall we go? Speed is everything

now. When our work's done, we'll have time for sleep
and rest.

Neoptolemos
As soon as this head wind drops, then we'll leave. At
the moment it stands in the wrong quarter.

Philoctetes
For a voyage out of harm's way any wind is good.

Neoptolemos
I know, but this blows just as hard against them.

Philoctetes
Give a bandit the chance to rob and plunder, and no
wind blows against him.

Neoptolemos
As you're determined, then, we leave. Will you need
anything or want anything from your cave?

Philoctetes
There isn't much, but some things I must have with me.

Neoptolemos
Things you won't find on my ship?

Philoctetes
Yes, leaves that keep this wound from erupting. They
give me great relief.

Neoptolemos
Bring them, then. What else do you want to take?

Philoctetes
Any arrows I may have forgotten. Nothing must be left
lying for someone to find when we've gone.

Neoptolemos
And that is the bow which they say no one and nothing
can resist?

Philoctetes
Yes, here in my hands, this is the great bow of Hercules.

Neoptolemos
May I look more closely? Am I allowed to feel its power,
do reverence to that power, place my hands where
Hercules placed his?

Philoctetes
Yes, boy, you are allowed. Command anything of mine
if it will serve your purpose.

Neoptolemos
I long to touch it, but only on one condition—that I

break no sacred law. If I do, say no more.

Philoctetes

No, you break no law. Your words come from a pure heart. You saved me from the darkness, boy, through you I breathe again, I live. I will see the earth of my homeland again, my old father, my friends . . . through you. My enemies were all around me and you snatched me out of their reach . . . You must have no fear. You will be allowed to hold this bow, give it back, then say— I alone, I, Neoptolemos, out of the whole world, have been permitted to touch the bow of Hercules—that will be your boast. And you deserve it, you are a good man. I won the bow through doing good; so will you.

Neoptolemos

Go inside . . . We must hurry . . .

Philoctetes

Let me take you. Here . . . [*He leans on* NEOPTOLEMOS.] My disease makes me like a child. See how I depend on you.

[*Exit* PHILOCTETES *and* NEOPTOLEMOS.

Sailors

I have seen many people in pain, have heard of their suffering, their torture. But I know only one doomed more cruelly than this man. He was Ixion. And I never saw this, only heard . . . but they say he was broken and bound to a giant wheel, turning, turning, in endless agony. But that was punishment. Ixion tried to defile the union of the greatest power in the universe, tried to part Zeus and his bride.

Philoctetes hurt no one, robbed no one,

Philoctetes gave as he received,

A straight rule runs through his soul,

Yet he is destroyed, crushed.

And the mystery is, how he clung to life, alone,
     the only sound the great waves surging,

The rocks for silent company, a cripple.

He shrieked in agony—no one came, no one heard . . .

The pain's jaws sink deep, the blood swells up,
     steaming,

There is no one, no one to stop the flow with gentle
     leaves, gathered from the cool earth . . .

And his foot rages like a beast, the wound flares,
    and in its heart the poison seethes.
Given peace from the curse that consumed his
    being, he would creep from place to place,
Tottering like an infant without its nurse,
He would search for food, hope it was near . . .
But in this barren land no corn grows, and no one
    came to trade with him.
He filled his stomach with flesh from birds, killed in
    full flight by his faithful arrows.
Ten years and the poor wretch never had the taste
    of wine glittering out of a cup.
The rain left pools between the rocks, and he found
    those, scooped up the water, and survived.
But now he's met Neoptolemos, son of kings, and
    his fortune changes.
After all he's endured, he rises, great, strong,
Sails home in our ship.
The months of his agony end. Our leader takes him
    to the shores of Melias, where the nymphs play,
    to the banks of the Spercheios,
Where Hercules, the hero of the bronze shield, joined
    the great company of heaven, all ablaze over the
    slopes of Oeta in the divine fire of his father,
    Zeus.

[*Enter* NEOPTOLEMOS.

Neoptolemos
[*Into the cave.*] Quickly, then, if you want to . . . Philoctetes! [*Enter* PHILOCTETES. *He stops, unable to speak.*]
Can't you speak . . . ? [*Silence.*] Are you turned to stone
or . . . Philoctetes! [*A sound comes from* PHILOCTETES,
but it is not articulate.] What is it?

Philoctetes
[*Suppressing the signs of the pain.*] Nothing! No cause
. . . for alarm . . . [*He makes the effort.*] Come, let's
start, boy.

Neoptolemos
Do you feel your wound? Is there pain now?

Philoctetes
No, no, not at all. No, I feel the pain less . . . God in
heaven . . . !

Neoptolemos
Why call on heaven?

Philoctetes
I call on heaven to save me . . . And heal me. [*Another sound is forced out of him.*]

Neoptolemos
What's happened to you? Tell me . . . You must! What's wrong—you can't hide it!

Philoctetes
It's killing me, boy, I can't . . . the foul thing's killing me. Look, I . . . Oh, it's coming now . . . ! [*He gives another cry.*] Right through me, right through, I can't . . . the torture, it . . . death! Eaten alive, boy, *eaten* . . . ! [*He shrieks, a long drawn-out shriek of agony.*] Dear god! . . . Get your sword out, boy. Cut . . . there, cut the foot off . . . Now! Hurry! Chop it away. Don't care if I die . . . Come *on*, boy!

Neoptolemos
One moment—silence, then, without warning, these sounds, this screaming. I can't see the cause . . .

Philoctetes
You know, boy.

Neoptolemos
I don't.

Philoctetes
You *know!*

Neoptolemos
What is it? I don't know.

Philoctetes
Why not? You must! [*He screams again.*]

Neoptolemos
The poison . . . I see . . . working in you now . . . it's terrible . . .

Philoctetes
Terrible, boy, I can't tell you . . . pity me.

Neoptolemos
What shall I do?

Philoctetes
Wait, don't be afraid. Stay with me. It goes, but it comes back, after a time . . . always . . .

Neoptolemos

[*In tears.*] My friend, to see you suffering, I . . . all this suffering . . . Do you want me to lift you? . . . Here . . . I'll carry you . . .

Philoctetes

No, no, don't! Here, take the bow—you asked me just now—take it till this attack lets me go. Safely, mind you, guard it. When the pain leaves I must sleep—I get no relief otherwise. Don't wake me, let me sleep on. If Odysseus and the others come before I wake don't, in the name of all that's sacred, don't let that bow leave your hands—whatever he tries to make you do, even if you want to—and don't let him trick you. Otherwise we'll both be corpses. I give you my life. Guard it.

Neoptolemos

I will, Philoctetes, depend on me. I'll keep watch, and the bow will never leave me till it returns to you. Give it to me—and may good come of our work today.

[PHILOCTETES *at last hands over the bow.*

Philoctetes

There, in your hands, boy. Pray god it's power, the spirit of death it carries, never brings you my agony— or the labors it brought Hercules.

Neoptolemos

Heaven grant that prayer. And grant us all a safe and prosperous voyage, wherever our destiny and our mission take us.

Philoctetes

I'm afraid, boy, afraid your prayer may wither as soon as you say it . . . Look, the wound's a pit of blood now, scarlet. That's from deep in the flesh . . . Pulse, pulse . . . I can feel it coming . . . worse again . . . ! [*He groans.*] That foot, the crimes it commits on me! Coming now . . . getting closer . . . No, don't, no, I can't—Yes, boy, look, now you have it all, HERE! . . . No, don't leave me . . . [*He screams.*] Odysseus, if only this agony would rip your breast apart! [*He screams again.*] And you generals, Agamemnon and Menelaus, both of you, just you nurse this disease as long as I have . . . Oh no, please . . . help me . . . Death! Death! Every day I call on you—

why can you never come to me? . . . My boy, dear
friend, kind . . . friend, take me to the mountaintop, to
the pit of lava there, and burn me in it . . . kind friend
. . . I did so much for Hercules, and my reward was the
bow you're holding now . . . What do you say, boy, what
do you say? . . . Why don't you speak? What are you
thinking?

Neoptolemos

Of your agony . . . all this time . . . it's terrible to watch.
Look, I weep, Philoctetes . . .

Philoctetes

Yes, boy, but we must have strength. When the pain
comes it breaks me. But it soon goes. All I ask from
you is, don't leave me alone, not alone!

Neoptolemos

Trust our promise. We stay.

Philoctetes

Will *you* stay?

Neoptolemos

Of course. You know I will.

Philoctetes

I would be ashamed to make you swear, boy . . .

Neoptolemos

I cannot leave this island without you. I'm bound to
stay—it is my duty.

Philoctetes

I believe you . . . Give me your hand.

Neoptolemos

There, my hand in yours . . . I stay.

Philoctetes

I must . . . I . . . up there . . .

Neoptolemos

Where?

Philoctetes

Up . . . !

Neoptolemos

You're in a fever. Why look up there? Only the sky's up
there.

Philoctetes

Let me go, let me *go!*

Neoptolemos
Where to?

Philoctetes
Let me go, can't you?

Neoptolemos
I won't leave you . . .

Philoctetes
You kill me every time you touch me!

[NEOPTOLEMOS *lets go his hand.*

Neoptolemos
You're free. Your thoughts came clearer then.

Philoctetes
Earth, receive this . . . this rotting carcass . . . this . . .
thing . . . this . . . foul thing! I can't stand . . . I can't . . .
[*He collapses.*]

Neoptolemos
He'll sleep. Look, it won't be long. His head's lolling, his
whole body's drenched in sweat . . . This vein in his foot,
all black with poisoned blood, it's ruptured now . . .
Leave him, friends, don't disturb him. Let him sleep.

Sailors
Sleep, out of the reach of pain, out of the reach
     of sorrow,
Sleep, come down gently,
Come down sweetly smiling, smiling,
And master him.
Keep this beam of calm spread over his eyes,
Come to us here,
Come and heal him.
See where you have reached, boy, and where you
     must go.
Think, think what must follow.
Look, you see, we wait. We wait for you.
You will decide, but you must decide now. This
     is the moment, and you must grasp it.
The moment gives you power—
And asks for action.

Neoptolemos
He's unconscious—we have his bow. But we still lose all
if we sail without him. The final triumph belongs to him
—that is decreed in heaven—and we must bring him to

Troy; if the glorious outcome of all our lies is to admit
we failed, we are fools, we are criminals, and everyone
will know it!

Sailors

Heaven will decide the outcome, boy . . .

Next time you answer, make your voice small,
    small . . . When sick men sleep they keep an
    inner sentinel on watch . . .

Now—quietly—measure your hopes against the
    future and see where you stand.

If you persist with your plan—you know what I
    mean—no way out of the pain, the suffering
    . . . isn't it clear? Isn't it?

But the wind's in our favor, boy, in our favor. The
    man's stretched out there on his back, helpless,
    as good as blind . . .

Sleep in the sun will make him well . . .

Hands, feet, every muscle—idle, he lies there like one
    of the sleeping dead in their graves . . .

Careful, watch what you say, careful of your words
    now!

Choose.

But if you are wise, boy, choose the way that will
    bring us home safe . . .

That is the way that wins you victory.

Neoptolemos

Stop! Guard your words and watch him. He's awake,
his eyes moved . . . He's raising his head . . .

Philoctetes

Light—sun's shining . . . I've been asleep . . . The strangers!—Still there, watching, and I scarcely dared hope
. . . I prayed for this, boy, but I never believed . . . You
stayed, you had pity, watched over me, bore with the
filthy disease. Agamemnon and Menelaus, those two
brave generals, they couldn't bear it—no spirit to endure
such things. But you, boy, there is strength in you, the
strength of kings, and you made light of this, the
shrieking, the stench—all nothing to you . . . It's leaving
me a little, the pain, some peace from it now. Help me
up . . . No, you, boy, I want you to help me stand. Then
as soon as this exhaustion leaves me, we must get down

to your ship and start our journey.

Neoptolemos

I'm happy just to see you live, breathe, be free from pain—it seemed impossible. When you collapsed, we thought we were watching a man dying. Now, try to stand—or would you rather my men carried you? We have decided what must be done, and they will obey. They are not afraid.

Philoctetes

Thank you, boy, yes, lift me up, as you said. But don't ask your men to help—no need for them to suffer the nausea and the stench before they have to. Their work comes later, and they'll find it hard enough, living on the same ship with me.

Neoptolemos

As you wish. Stand up then. Hold on to me . . .

Philoctetes

Have courage, boy. My will learned long ago how to force me upright.

[NEOPTOLEMOS *breaks down.*

Neoptolemos

What am I to do? I can't go on!

Philoctetes

What is it, boy? . . . I couldn't follow then . . . what you said . . .

Neoptolemos

I don't know how . . . it's impossible. How can I find the words?

Philoctetes

What's impossible? Don't talk like that, boy.

Neoptolemos

I talk like that because I'm trapped. Trapped!

Philoctetes

You've changed your mind and I'm not to sail with you? It's my disease . . .

Neoptolemos

The whole world smells diseased, Philoctetes, when you betray all you ever stood for, choke back your conscience . . .

Philoctetes

You've betrayed nothing. You helped me. I am a good

man. Your father would have done the same, said the same . . .

Neoptolemos
Now I'll be famous—Neoptolemos the guilty, the soiled!
When I think of it, the shame burns me!

Philoctetes
No, not shame, not for anything you've done . . . As for
what you told me—yes, now I am afraid . . .

Neoptolemos
God in heaven tell me what to do! Doubly wrong,
doubly guilty. Hiding what I should have told him—
and then those squalid lies . . .

Philoctetes
Yes, I see now, it's all plain. I am the one he's betrayed.
He'll leave me behind, set sail for home.

Neoptolemos
Yes, set sail, but not leave you. No, what torments me is,
I'll take you, but the journey will be full of hate for you.

Philoctetes
What do you mean? I don't understand.

Neoptolemos
I'll hide nothing from you now . . . Philoctetes, on this
voyage, you are bound for Troy and the Greek army, the
army commanded by Agamemnon and Menelaus.

Philoctetes
No, it's not true!

Neoptolemos
Don't despair, before you've heard what I . . .

Philoctetes
What is there to hear? . . . Oh, what are you trying to
do to me?

Neoptolemos
To get you cured—first I'll do that. Then, we'll go out
together, Philoctetes, and we'll conquer Troy!

Philoctetes
And you believe you can succeed?

Neoptolemos
Great forces are at work in this war and we must give
way to them. Listen, and control your passion . . .

Philoctetes
A cruel murderous trick! . . . What have you done to

me, stranger? Give me back my bow—now, *now!*

Neoptolemos

Impossible. I have my duty—I have myself to think of.
I must obey my orders . . .

Philoctetes

You . . . fire! You all-consuming terror! You foul, schem-
ing, treacherous fiend! Think! Think what you've done,
think how you've lied. How can you bear to look at me,
after I begged you, went and groveled to you—don't
you sweat for shame . . . thief? . . . Taking my bow,
stealing my very life . . . Give the bow back, I'll do
anything, only give it back, please, please, boy. By all
that's holy to you, don't rob me of life itself. [NEOPTOLE-
MOS *is silent.* PHILOCTETES *groans.*] Not even a word
from him now. The bow is his, he means to keep it, so
he turns his back on me . . . Oh, my loyal, my only
friends, you shores and cliffs, you herds of mountain
animals, you rocky ravines, listen to me, listen, because
I don't know who else will ever listen—I'm calling to
you, *weeping!* See what this boy, this brat of Achilles,
see what he's done to me! He swears to take me home,
then takes me to Troy. He puts his hand in mine,
accepts the sacred weapons of Hercules from me, then
makes a present of them to the Greeks. He hauls me off,
as if he'd fought and conquered a mighty warrior. But
does he know what he's been fighting? The shell of a
man, a shadow of smoke, a corpse! If I had my own
strength back he would have no chance; even now, only
a trick gives him victory. Well, the trick has worked.
I'm the victim. What remains . . . ? Give back the bow,
you can still be true to yourself. What do you say? . . .
Silence. I see . . . Annihilation! . . . And so, I come back
to you, to my home. Once again I crawl into my tunnel
in the rock, naked, starving. Alone in my cave I shall
shrivel away. The birds in the air, the animals in the
mountains are safe from my bow. Instead, my rotting
carcase will gorge the beasts on which I once fed myself.
Yes, now the hunted become the hunters. I'll pay for my
murders in my own flesh, sentenced by a man who
seemed pure in heart . . . God curse you, and may you
. . . No, first, I ask you, just once more—will you change

your mind? If you say no, die and be damned to you!

Sailors

[*To* NEOPTOLEMOS:] What are your orders, sir? It is your decision. Do we sail? Or do we take the way he shows us?

Neoptolemos

All I know is, the pity ... when I see him ... the terrible pity I feel. I can't put it out of my mind.

Philoctetes

For the love of heaven have mercy, boy! Go on with this deceit and your name will be a foul word everywhere. Don't let that happen.

Neoptolemos

I can't decide, I ... if only I'd never left Skyros. All this weighs on me, I can't think ...

Philoctetes

There is good in you but it is being corrupted. You have taken instruction from someone else, someone evil. Learn from better teachers, give me back my bow, and sail out of here.

Neoptolemos

What should we do, men?

[*Enter* ODYSSEUS, *with a force of* SOLDIERS.

Odysseus

You fool, what are you doing, you'll kill us all! Give me that bow and get back to the ship!

Philoctetes

Who's there? ... I heard Odysseus ...

Odysseus

You heard right. Odysseus ... And now you see him.

Philoctetes

Yes, I do see—I've been sold for slaughter. So he trapped me; he robbed me of my bow.

Odysseus

Guilty. I admit everything.

Philoctetes

[*To* NEOPTOLEMOS:] Give it back, boy—here, quick. The bow. The bow!

Odysseus

No, Philoctetes, he may like to, but he never will. And you must come with us ... Or must we use force?

Philoctetes
Force! That suits you! That satisfies you! Yes, you've reached that low.

Odysseus
Well, if you refuse to move yourself . . .

Philoctetes
Earth of Lemnos, you all-consuming jets of fire gushing out of the forge of Hephaestes—do you let such things go on? Do you let Odysseus drag me, force me from your island?

Odysseus
The power that rules this island is Zeus, do you understand? Zeus decreed what must happen. And I am the servant of Zeus.

Philoctetes
You turn my stomach, pretending that god is on your side. Oh, your clever philosophy! You make god tell lies!

Odysseus
No, god tells the truth. Our way is clear. It must be traveled.

Philoctetes
Never!

Odysseus
I say it must. And you will obey.

Philoctetes
Oh yes, yes, I see now, I've lost my freedom. My state in life is to be a slave.

Odysseus
You're wrong. You will be one of the heroes of Troy. In their company you will take the city and destroy it.

Philoctetes
Never! Never! Do what you like, I don't care what happens, so long as one cliff on this island rises high enough . . .

Odysseus
What would you do?

Philoctetes
Throw myself over—now—dash my brains out—the rocks below—give them blood . . .

[PHILOCTETES *struggles toward the edge of a cliff.*]

Odysseus

Hold him! Don't let him move!

[ODYSSEUS's *men reach* PHILOCTETES *just in time and pin him down.*

Philoctetes

My arms, now you need the bow you loved, now, when this marauder springs his trap . . . Odysseus, have you ever, in all your life, had a single pure or honest thought? You stalk me like an animal, hunt me down, skulking out of sight behind a boy I couldn't recognize. He's too good for you, he's worth something . . . he should be following me. But what does he know about anything except obeying orders? Look at him now. Disgusted with the lies he's had to tell, the suffering I've been through . . . He was innocent, he didn't like your methods. But you, with your instinct for the tortuous, the crooked, the twisted, you closed in on him, and taught him how to operate like you, how to be clever like you. So now, you miserable creature, you've made your capture and you mean to haul me off. But you flung me on this very beach—don't you remember—years ago, without a friend, without a possession, without a home—a walking corpse! . . . Heaven strike you dead! Over and over again I've prayed for your death, but heaven never allows me any pleasure and you live on, serene and happy, while I curse life for bringing me nothing but pain and sorrow. Yes, you laugh at me, don't you—you and your two generals? Now you run their errands, you servile official. But you joined them in the beginning only because you had no choice. You were tricked into coming while, I, god, when I think of it! I brought seven ships, I sailed myself—and then they leave me here to rot! . . . Or so you say—but they blame *you*. Why not just forget me? Why drag me back to life? What can you possibly hope for? I'm nothing to you, I died long ago. Can't you see, you devil, I'm lame, I stink! . . . How are you going to offer sacrifices to heaven with me on board? Will the wine you pour be sacred?—That was your excuse when you threw me off your ship ten years ago . . . May you all die in agony. And if there is justice left in the world, you will die, you will, for the things you've done to me. But I know there is justice, I know that heaven cares. You were driven here. Nothing less than the will of a higher power would bring you on a journey like this—for me, a wreck of a man . . . Oh, you land of my fathers and you powers that watch over it, take vengeance, vengeance on every last one of them—however late, however delayed—but in the name of pity I must have vengeance. My life is torment, but if I live to see them destroyed, I'll think I've got the cure for my disease.

Sailors

His words crush us all, Odysseus. There was no sign of yielding. In spite of all, the stranger will not give way.

Odysseus

If I could afford an argument now I would have a reply to every word of that. As it is, my defence is simply this. I am what the time and the circumstance ask me to be. When they demand just and upright men you will find no one with a stronger sense of duty than myself. But whatever I do, I must succeed, I must. I was born so . . . And yet, your case is an exception. I intend —no, I choose—to leave you as you are . . . [*To* SOLDIERS:] Let him go, no one is to touch him. He can stay here. [*To* PHILOCTETES:] We have the bow, we don't need you as well. Teukros is with us, he knows how to use it. Or myself. I think I could master it as well as you. I can aim, I can shoot. Why do you have to be there at all? Goodbye—and enjoy your walks on Lemnos. [*To the others*:] Come, we leave now. [*To* PHILOCTETES:] Perhaps the bow you were lucky enough to own will bring me some glory. Remember, it should have been yours.

Philoctetes

What am I to do? It's cruel . . . I can't . . . So now you swagger back to the Greek army, show off my bow . . .

Odysseus

No, Philoctetes, no discussion, nothing, because I'm going.

Philoctetes

Son of Achilles, are you leaving too, just like that, without a word? Can't I speak to you either?

Odysseus

[*To* NEOPTOLEMOS:] Come. Quickly. Don't look. You have
fine feelings, but I know those feelings—they could ruin
our chances.

Philoctetes

[*To* SAILORS:] My friends, am I to be left here? Alone? Not
one of you has any pity on me?

Sailors

He commands us, this young man here. Whatever he
says to you, we say.

Neoptolemos

Odysseus will tell me that pity, only pity, moves me . . .
But I was born so! [*To* SAILORS:] Stay, if he wants you
—but only so long as we take to fit out the ship and
pray for a good voyage. Perhaps by then he will have
thought. He may soften, and that would help us. [*To*
ODYSSEUS:] Let's leave them, then . . . [*To* SAILORS:]
When we call you, back on board immediately.

[*Exeunt* NEOPTOLEMOS, ODYSSEUS, *and the* SOLDIERS.

Philoctetes

My rock, my hollow, my retreat, my fire and frost—you
see we are doomed to each other, you and I, for all time.
You will watch me dying . . . Oh, no, no, no . . . You
walls, you've drunk in my tears of pain—now my days
will be empty, all hope gone, life withering . . . Fly up
there, you pigeons. The air is yours again. I can't
touch you.

Sailors

Whatever happens now, however terrible, however
harsh, remember it is your doing, it is your sentence on
yourself. No greater power decides. You were offered
help and hope. You chose suffering.

Philoctetes

I am afraid, afraid. The sickness and pain weigh on
me, bury me. The lonely days will pass, and the end of
my stay will come in death . . . [*He weeps.*] Never find
food again, never hold my arrows in my hands again
. . . my strong hands, well hands . . . Lies! Deceit! They
told me lies and their minds—cunning, oh cunning—got
me! I never thought he'd . . . Let him suffer, only let

him suffer for that. Let him find out how it feels, the
years, the years, the years . . .

Sailors

It wasn't lies put you in our power.

It was the destiny that guides this war, that gives
    our struggle purpose.

Save your curses for others, they have a bitter sound,
    they bring ill luck.

All we ask, all we expect is—accept our friendship.

Philoctetes

Think of it, oh, just think of it, at this moment he's
sitting on the beach, the sea's gray and foaming, and
he's laughing, waving it in his hands—my life, my only
hope of life . . . And no one in the world ever touched
it before . . . Oh, my bow, my dear bow, wrenched out
of my hands, so dear to you, look, here I am—you understand, you have feelings, my bow—here I am, the friend
of Hercules, the one he trusted, and never, never again
do I have the use of you. Now you've a new master, so
clever, endlessly clever, you'll see his mind at work, in-
venting . . . I hate him, I loathe him, that man, breeding
his crimes . . . and what he did to me, the foul,
detestable . . .

Sailors

As a man, you must say—I believe this is right . . .

But when you do—

Not in anger;

Not spitting abuse;

Not wounding.

Odysseus was one man, given orders by a whole
    army, and he obeyed.

All he did was serve his people, help his friends.

Philoctetes

Fly up there, you birds! Every beast of the field, turn
your bright eyes here. Come down from the mountains,
out of your hiding places, no need to leap away in
terror. Look, empty. My hands are empty. No bow, no
power any more. I'm weak now, forget your fear, there's
no danger here for you, come near . . . You'll have justice now, fill your stomachs with my rotting flesh—I'll
soon be carrion. From nothing there can be no life. I'll

have nothing from the earth, nothing from my bow—
and will the winds nourish me?

Sailors

In heaven's name, friendship is sacred, a treasure. We
Bring you friendship—embrace it, hug it to you.
But remember—and let this be clear—
You can escape, nothing holds you to this suffering . . .
Unless it is yourself,
Feeding your sorrow on bitterness,
Keeping it alive with your own tears,
Making it your only friend.

Philoctetes

Of all who ever came here, you have been the best,
the kindest, and yet even you bring me back to my
agony, again, again. Why did you do this to me, why
did you destroy me?

Sailors

What do you mean?

Philoctetes

Troy is everything I hate, yet you thought you would
take me there.

Sailors

Because we believe that is best.

Philoctetes

Then leave me alone, leave me now!

Sailors

You've given us our wish.
We obey willingly, willingly.
Come, our ship is waiting, let's go to her now.

Philoctetes

No, wait, in the name of heaven, you swore. Don't
go, don't go!!

Sailors

Gently . . . gently . . .

Philoctetes

Friends, stay with me, for god's sake!

Sailors

Why call us back?

Philoctetes

AIAI, AIAI,
My life, all my life . . .

Gone from me . . . spent . . .
You, you, my foot—can I bear you with me now? . . .
Friends, come here, come back, come back again . . . !

Sailors

And if we do, what shall we change? What will be
different?
Your purpose is fixed, you showed it.
Can you alter now?

Philoctetes

Don't be angry with me. The grief's a storm, it drowns
me. I'm driven mad, I rave.

Sailors

Come, then. You have no other hope, do what we tell
you.

Philoctetes

Never, never! I stay here, fixed, firm. Let the lightning
come, let the thunderbolt strike me, let fire and flame
burn me up—I will not go. Troy can sink in its own
damnation, and the whole army with it! . . . They flung
me aside, no remorse, left my tortured limbs to rot here
. . . Friends, wait, do one thing for me, look, I'm plead-
ing for it . . .

Sailors

What do you mean?

Philoctetes

A sword, someone, an axe, anything sharp, get me . . .

Sailors

Why? What for? What do you want to do?

Philoctetes

Cut the flesh from my limbs, the flesh—myself—with
my . . . the mind's murdering now, murdering . . . !

Sailors

Why . . . ?

Philoctetes

I'll find my father, I'll go to him . . .

Sailors

Where, where will you find him?

Philoctetes

In the grave, never in the sunlight! . . . Oh, my city,
my country, my home—I want to see you, I want to see
you again. The fool that I was, leaving you, sailing out

from your shore to help the Greeks, the damned faithless
Greeks! . . . Nothing . . . I'm nothing now . . . [*He turns
and goes back into his cave.*]

Sailors

We would be with our ship now, we would have
   left you already, Philoctetes . . .
But we saw Odysseus, and the son of Achilles in the
   distance. They're coming back . . .

[*Enter* NEOPTOLEMOS, *followed by* ODYSSEUS.

Odysseus

I want the reason, Neoptolemos. You turn back, you give
no warning, start to run—run all the way . . .

Neoptolemos

I've done wrong. I mean to make it right.

Odysseus

Yes, it's terrible to do wrong. But what was your fault?

Neoptolemos

Odysseus, when I did what you and our army asked of
me . . .

Odysseus

You did your duty. Be proud of yourself!

Neoptolemos

I used lies, I used deceit to trap a man—and that makes
me ashamed.

Odysseus

Trap a man . . . ? Now, wait, boy, think, take care!

Neoptolemos

Yes, I'll take care! I'll take care that Philoctetes . . .

Odysseus

Now you frighten me. What are you going to do?

Neoptolemos

. . . Philoctetes, from whom I took this bow, will once
more . . .

Odysseus

No! You can't give it back. By all that's sacred, you can't!

Neoptolemos

I have no right to the bow. I got it by a lie.

Odysseus

God in heaven, this is some cruel joke of yours. It must
be!

Neoptolemos

Right—if you think the truth a joke.

Odysseus

I don't understand you, boy. Do you know what you're saying?

Neoptolemos

I told you. Must I repeat it and repeat it . . .

Odysseus

I wish I'd never heard it once, I tell you that!

Neoptolemos

Good. Then all is clear? Quite understood?

Odysseus

There's a power that can stop you . . . Oh yes, there is, I assure you.

Neoptolemos

Who? Who will stop me?

Odysseus

The armies of all Greece . . . Myself, since I act for them.

Neoptolemos

You were born with brains. Use them when you speak.

Odysseus

No, boy—*you* talk brainless. And you act brainless, too.

Neoptolemos

But I have right on my side, and that is stronger than your brains.

Odysseus

What do you mean, right? I planned this, I got you the bow, and now you hand it back.

Neoptolemos

I've done wrong. I am ashamed. I'm trying to make up for that wrong.

Odysseus

Think of the Greek army . . . Can you still do it? Not afraid?

Neoptolemos

Why be afraid? I do right.

Odysseus

But I am here to say you do wrong—and prove it.

Neoptolemos

Your threats prove nothing to me, Odysseus.

Odysseus

It won't be Troy we go to war against, but you.

Neoptolemos

So be it.

Odysseus

You see where my right hand is resting—on my sword.

Neoptolemos

Look, I follow you, I'm ready . . .

[*Pause.*

Odysseus

No, I won't prevent you. But I'll go and tell them in the Greek army what you've done—and the army, boy, will have your blood! [*Exit* ODYSSEUS.]

Neoptolemos

Very wise. Always be as careful as this in future, and you may spare yourself some painful injuries. [NEOPTOLEMOS *turns toward the cave.*] Philoctetes! . . . Are you there in the cave? . . . Come out here, leave that place.

[*Enter* PHILOCTETES.

Philoctetes

What was the noise? I heard shouting . . . Why call me out again? Do you need me . . . friends! . . . Look what you've done. Haven't you brought enough suffering—or have you found a new way of tormenting me?

Neoptolemos

Don't be afraid. Listen, I've something to say . . .

Philoctetes

I *am* afraid. Once before you had something to say—and such honesty. I listened then—and suffered for it.

Neoptolemos

Can no one change, feel remorse? Is it never possible?

Philoctetes

And that was how you sounded when you were stealing my bow. The words I could trust. But the man behind them—he destroyed me.

Neoptolemos

That's not so, not now. I want you to tell me, are you decided? Do you stay here, whatever happens, or do you sail with us and . . .

Philoctetes

No, no, you can talk, you can say what you like, it's
useless!

Neoptolemos

And so you are determined?

Philoctetes

More than I can hope to say.

Neoptolemos

I wanted to persuade you, I had the words ready but . . .
they are all wrong, I can't . . . That finishes it, then.

Philoctetes

Good. You would only waste your words. You will never
make me your friend . . . Trick me out of life itself,
leave me destitute, then you come and lecture me . . .
Oh, your father was all goodness, but his son—shame,
shame! Damn you everlastingly, Agamemnon, Menelaus,
Odysseus, all of you . . .

Neoptolemos

Stop your cursing . . . Here, take the bow, it's yours.

Philoctetes

How do you mean? . . . Is this another trick?

Neoptolemos

I swear by the supreme godhead of almighty Zeus . . .

Philoctetes

You mean it—then I'm safe . . . This is the truth now?

Neoptolemos

Actions are truth, they tell no lies. Watch . . . Give me
your right hand. Now, be master of your bow again.

[*Enter* ODYSSEUS, *with* SOLDIERS.

Odysseus

But I say no—in the name of god, who sees and remembers all, on behalf of the Greek generals and the
allied army . . . !

Philoctetes

Who said that, boy? Odysseus—that was Odysseus!

Odysseus

Yes, I have come for you, Philoctetes. I am taking you
back to the plains of Troy by force, whether the son of
Achilles wishes it or not.

Philoctetes

But not alive . . . [PHILOCTETES *snatches the bow and*

raises it.] . . . if this bow aims true . . .

[NEOPTOLEMOS *leaps forward to grab his arm.*

Neoptolemos

No! Don't—stop! For the love of heaven, don't shoot!

Philoctetes

Let me go! Dear god, let go my arm!

Neoptolemos

I will *not* let go!

[*While* PHILOCTETES *struggles to free himself,* ODYSSEUS *makes good his escape.*

Philoctetes

Look, why stop me? I could have killed him—my worst enemy, the man I hate most in the world—in the range of my bow—and you stop me . . .

Neoptolemos

Killing him does no good—to either of us.

Philoctetes

Well, I tell you this much—the generals of that army, the lying so-called heralds of the Greeks, they're cowards in a fight, you see, only brave so long as they talk!

Neoptolemos

Perhaps. So now you have your bow—and no reason to be angry with me, no reason to blame me.

Philoctetes

You're right. You've shown your father's spirit, boy. Your father, when he was alive he was admitted to be our greatest warrior and now . . . now he is the greatest of the dead.

Neoptolemos

When a man such as you speaks well of my father and myself it makes me proud. But listen, Philoctetes, I want something from you, and I'm determined to have it . . . Many things that happen in life are the work of greater powers, forces we cannot control; those we must accept. But some misfortunes we wish upon ourselves, and if a person broods on these, as you do, he deserves no indulgence, no pity. You are like a wild animal now—you won't reason, you won't talk; if someone, trying to help, gives you advice, you go to war at once, and attack him in fury. Nevertheless, I'll say it—

and you must listen to this because I call Zeus to witness—so chisel it in your brain . . . You are sick and in pain for a reason. No man willed it, eternal powers directed it. You trespassed on sacred ground. On that ground a snake, guardian of the sanctuary, lay coiled, waiting in the darkness. You must realize that you will find no cure for the disease that is destroying you—no, never, not while the sun rises in the east and sets in the west—unless you go of your own free will to the battlefields of Troy. There you must find the sons of Asclepius, they are there in our army, and let them heal your wounds. You must then help me break the resistance of our enemies with your bow. This is the truth. And I will tell you how I know it. One of our prisoners from Troy is Helenus—a great prophet there. He has told us, and we cannot doubt it, that all this is bound to happen. And what is more, he said that Troy is destined to fall this coming summer. He is willing to forfeit his life if he's proved wrong. Now you know everything, Philoctetes. Come with us and come willingly. The reward . . . oh, it's a great, it's a fine reward—to be a hero, the only Greek, the best of all, to find doctors who will heal you, and then, above all, to win eternal glory for yourself by taking the city of Troy, the cause of so much sorrow.

Philoctetes

Life, my torturer, why, oh why keep me here on earth, why not let me sink into darkness and death? What can I do? How can I ignore what he said—it was said out of a good heart, to help me. And yet, am I so weak? . . . Say I go. How do I walk among people again, or speak to them? How could you, my eyes, having watched all that has happened to me, bear to see me keeping company with my murderers, Agamemnon and Menelaus— or with the all-corrupting Odysseus? The agonies I've suffered in the past—they can't hurt me now—but thinking of what those men could still do to me—that can, yes, it can. A man's first crime is like a mother; it trains him, fosters him to be evil all his life . . . One thing in you surprises me. You have a duty—keep away from Troy, keep me away. They robbed you, stole your father's armor. And now will you go and take the side of the thieves, and force me to do the same? No, never, my boy. No, do what you promised, promised on oath, and take me home. Stay in Skyros yourself, leave them all to perish as they deserve, mercilessly defeated. For that, I'll thank you and so will my father—you see, a double reward. Side with evil and you wear its mask, you begin to be what you have sided with. Don'tl

Neoptolemos
I know you are in the right. And yet I still want you to trust heaven and what I've told you. I am your friend. Sail out of this place with me ...

Philoctetes
To Troy? Is that it? Lame and crippled like this! To the Greek generals, to my most hated enemies ... ?

Neoptolemos
To those who will stop this gangrene in your foot, draw out your sickness, free you from pain ...

Philoctetes
And those terrible words are your advice? Do you know what you're asking?

Neoptolemos
Yes, and out of this the best will come. I see no other way for you, Philoctetes, or for me.

Philoctetes
Heaven listens when you say that. Do you feel no shame?

Neoptolemos
Why be ashamed to help my friend?

Philoctetes
What do you mean—help? Help me—or the Greek generals?

Neoptolemos
You, of course, because you're my friend. Everything I say shows that.

Philoctetes
Does it? Don't you want to betray me to my enemies?

Neoptolemos
My friend, please, listen! You are in great danger, learn not to be so proud, give way!

Philoctetes

You'll kill me, I know you, talking like this, you'll kill me!

Neoptolemos

No, no! I say you refuse to learn!

Philoctetes

I've learned, boy, I know my lesson. The Greek generals marooned me here!

Neoptolemos

But can't you see, those very people can save your life . . .

Philoctetes

Never! If being saved means going to Troy—I'll die!

Neoptolemos

What's to be done, then. I can't make you listen to me, I don't have the words. The easiest way is for me to spare my breath and for you to go on living as you live now—without hope of cure.

Philoctetes

My suffering is ordained—leave me to suffer. You promised to take me home, you gave me your hand on it—so do that for me and waste no more time by reminding me of Troy. Enough has been heard of Troy. My cries have sung its praises too many times.

Neoptolemos

If you're decided, let us go.

Philoctetes

At last I hear your father speaking . . .

Neoptolemos

Trust your good leg. Try to walk.

Philoctetes

There's just enough strength in me, I think.

Neoptolemos

[*Stopping.*] The Greeks will say I am wrong. How shall I defend myself?

Philoctetes

Don't think of it.

Neoptolemos

But if they attack, overrun my country . . .

Philoctetes

I will be there.

Neoptolemos
What help can you bring?

Philoctetes
The bow of Hercules.

Neoptolemos
How do you mean?

Philoctetes
I will keep away all invaders.

Neoptolemos
Say goodbye to the island . . . Then come.

[*The Spirit of* HERCULES *appears to them.*

Hercules
Not yet. First, listen to me . . . I speak to you, Philoctetes. The voice you hear, the vision you see, say they belong to Hercules. My place in heaven is empty, I walk on earth—for your sake, to show you the way your life must take, as Zeus designs it, and to halt the journey you are starting . . . Attend, attend to what I say. Before all, remember my destiny—the labors I went through, the sacrifices I made, and the end of all—honor from goodness without self. You see, such goodness never dies, such things never can. And to you, I tell you now, the same reward is due. Out of your labors here you will dress your life in glory. You will go to Troy with this man, and there be cured of your terrible disease; then you will be chosen first in valor, first in honor, first in goodness out of Greece; using my bow you will end the life of Paris, origin of all this suffering; you will crush Troy, send home costly trophies of your victory, and take the best, the richest spoil out of all the army, take them to your father and your lands in Oeta. But all that treasure, Philoctetes, must be brought to my burial place, to stand as memorial of my bow . . . Now, Neoptolemos, hear my words too. You have no power to take the land of Troy without Philoctetes, and he has none without you. Like two lions in the same country he guards you and you guard him . . . [*To* PHILOCTETES:] I will direct Asclepius to Troy, he will end your sickness. Then, for the second time, Troy will be taken by my bow. It is destined. But when you have the country at your mercy, helpless, destroyed, you must respect all

things sacred. Zeus, father of the universe, places nothing higher than this respect. Justice follows man through life and into death. Whether he lives or dies, justice remains, right is eternal, duty must be done.

Philoctetes

I longed to hear your voice, and now you have spoken, you have come to me, after so long, so long. I shall do your will. You are my master.

Neoptolemos

I stand with him. I am determined.

Hercules

Then hurry, you are late, you must start. The time is now, the voyage is before you, the wind set fair . . . GO!

[*The vision vanishes.*

Philoctetes

Now, as I leave, I call on my island to listen . . . This is where I lived, this was my mansion, where I lay, watching, watching—goodbye to you . . . Over there, the meadows and streams with their spirits of the water—goodbye, you spirits . . . Listen, the roar of the sea pounding on the rocks . . . the spray from those breakers often wet my hair as I lay in my cave—goodbye to the sea . . . Up there, the mountain of Hermes . . . you sent me echoes of my grief when the storm engulfed me—goodbye, goodbye. I am leaving you, I am leaving the springs where the sacred water rises, yes, now, though I never believed this day would come. Goodbye, island of Lemnos, sea-washed Lemnos, and send me on my journey with your blessing—no regrets, no blame—send me where the great power of my destiny wills, where the resolve of my friends, and the all-conquering spirit of my master, Hercules, carry me. He has decided. Now it must be done!

Sailors

Hurry . . .
Down to the ship . . .
Quickly, all of you . . .
Pray to the spirits of the sea before we leave . . .
Pray for a safe voyage home.

[*Exeunt, leaving Lemnos empty.*

—Translated by Kenneth Cavander